Contemporary COOKING

Volume 12

Contemporary
COOKING

Volume 12

Contemporary Cooking

Editorial production by James Charlton Associates, Ltd.,
New York. Editor-in-Chief, James Charlton; Executive Edi-
tor, Cara DeSilva; Managing Editors, Barbara Binswanger,
Jennie McGregor; Food Editors, Gilda Abramowitz, Helen
Feingold, Judy Knipe, Inez M. Krech, Betsy Lawrence,
Anne Lanigan, Maria Robbins, Susan Sarao, Joan
Whitman; Wine Consultant, Rory Callahan.

Book production and manufacturing consulting by:
Cobb/Dunlop Publishing Services, Inc., New York
Art Direction and interior design by:
Marsha Cohen/Parallelogram
Layout by: Jeanne Borczuk of SOHO Studio, New York
Composition by: Kachina Typesetting, Tempe, Arizona
Cover design by: Koechel/Peterson Design, Minneapolis

Acknowledgments: Pat Cocklin, Delu PAL International,
Alan Duns, John Elliott, Gus Francisco Photography, Mel-
vin Grey, Gina Harris, Anthony Kay, Paul Kemp, David
Levin, David Meldrum, Roger Phillips, Nick Powell, Iain
Reid, John Turner, Paul Williams, George Wright, Cuisin-
arts, Inc.

Printed and bound in Yugoslavia by CGP Delo.

Library of Congress Cataloging in Publication Data
Main entry under title:

Contemporary Cooking.

  Includes index.
  1. Cookery. I. Minnesota Mining and Manufacturing
Company.
TX715.C7586   1984   641.5   84-2563
0-88159-500-4   —   (set)
ISBN: 0-88159–011–8

CONTENTS
for the Contemporary Cooking Series

VOLUME 12

Part One

PIZZA, CALZONE AND FOCACCIA

"Believe it or not, Americans eat 75 *acres* of pizza a day!"
Boyd Matson
NBC News
February 6, 1985

In the years since World War II pizza has become as familiar to Americans as hot dogs and hamburgers, some say because many GI's developed a taste for it in Italy. In any case, the enormous demand has resulted in a mass-produced and highly uniform tomato and cheese pie—a far cry from the invariably fresh and highly varied Italian dish.

The first pizzas were rather crude flat breads, baked under the ashes of the cook fire. The Latin phrase *panus focus,* which translates roughly as "bottom-of-the-hearth bread," survives to this day as *focaccia,* a very earthy type of pizza bread that is flavored with olive oil, salt and herbs. In northern Italy in about 1000 B.C., the Etruscans ate bread like this as a kind of edible wrapper for whatever food happened to be at hand.

In the south of Italy the influence was more Greek than Etruscan, and the Greeks, further advanced at bread making than most cultures, introduced the notion of putting other food on top of the bread before it was baked. They made round, flat breads with toppings that included oils, onions, garlic, herbs, olives and cheeses—quite recognizably pizza as we know it, though of course lacking tomatoes.

Lovers of Italian food are sometimes startled to hear that the tomato was unknown in Italy until the sixteenth century, when it reached there from Peru. These early tomatoes were bright yellow (*pomodoro,* Italian for tomato, means "golden apple") and were generally assumed to be poisonous, as indeed the leaves are. The first pizza with tomatoes had to wait another two hundred years until some brave but anonymous Neapolitan soul had the nerve to try them.

It is also odd that today's notion of the "classic" pizza combination, cheese and tomato, arose neither spontaneously nor very long ago. In 1889 a man named Raffaelo Esposito created a special commemorative pizza for Queen Margherita, with a topping of cheese, basil and tomato. His purpose was merely to create a likeness of the Italian flag, but in the process he invented the modern pizza.

The pizzeria as we know it in America is a unique institution. Often less than a restaurant, not really a snack bar, it is usually a highly informal gathering place where hearty and sustaining food can be had cheaply and quickly. As such, it is yet another thing for which we can be grateful to the Neapolitans, for it was in Naples that the pizzeria originated and from there that it spread to America along with her emigrating sons and daughters.

The first pizzeria in America is said to have been opened sometime after the turn of the century by one Genaro Lombardi. That was on Spring Street in New York City, in the heart of the section known as Little Italy. Many others followed in Italian-American neighborhoods, but for most Americans pizza remained an exotic specialty until the end of World War II.

Inevitably, the pizza boom led to a proliferation of regional variations. New York pizza remains basically Neapolitan in style, with a thin crisp crust. Chicago pizza is a deep-dish pie with a thicker, heavier crust. California pizza, like California cuisine in general, tends to be experimental and eclectic, with unlikely ingredients like avocados or chilies thrown into the mix.

Of course, regional variations are not limited to America. In France, especially in the southeast, where the Italian influence is strongest, pizza is nearly as well loved as in Italy, though with a Gallic twist, of course. In Provence, pizza is based on fresh tomatoes, anchovies, olives, capers, pignolis (pine nuts) and garlic. The spicy Niçois version is an onion tart called pissaladière, topped with anchovies, olives and often herbs. When cheese is used on a pizza in France, it is not likely to be limited to mozzarella, but may include chèvre, Roquefort or Port-Salut, as well as any number of other cheeses from neighboring countries. And in Italy itself there is a variation called calzone, a crescent-shaped pizza turnover in which the topping has become a filling. It can be large so that one calzone serves 4, or it can be small to make individual portions.

Over the years pizza has proven to be one of the most varied and variable food we have. With good taste and a modicum of imagination, there is almost no limit to what it can be. In this spirit, homemade pizza is not just an imitation of the standard product, it is a return to the original idea.

PIZZA

There is nothing in the least mysterious or difficult about making delicious pizza in your own kitchen. With a minimum of planning, a pie can be assembled in minutes and be ready to eat half an hour later. While there are restaurants all over the country that specialize in making excellent, innovative and diverse pizzas, no commercial product available in the frozen food department of your supermarket, and no take-out pizza, stale and soggy by the time it reaches your plate, can rival the crisp, crusty freshness of your own home-baked pizza pie.

Ingredients

The basic and most important ingredient of any pizza is the crust. A simple bread dough is usually the choice for almost every variety of pizza, but you will certainly come across pizza pies that are made with a pastry dough crust and even a biscuit dough crust.

Unbleached All-Purpose Flour. This produces the most authentic Italian-style crust. It is widely available and very easy and pleasant to work with.

Whole-Wheat Flour. This produces a slightly stickier dough that bakes into a chewier, denser crust with a rich nutty flavor.

Semolina Flour. The hard durum wheat flour that is called for in making pasta can also be used to make pizza dough. It is slightly harder to work with because it lacks the elasticity of unbleached all-purpose flour, but it produces an extremely crisp pizza crust.

The only other ingredients necessary to make pizza dough are yeast, salt, olive oil and water.

Yeast. Use either fresh cake yeast or granulated active dry yeast. You may wish to review the section on Yeast Breads in Volume 7 for more detailed information on working with yeast.

Olive Oil. Olive oil not only makes the pizza dough more tender, but is an important flavoring agent as well. Buy the best olive oil you can afford.

Salt. Adjust the amount of salt called for in any recipe to complement the topping. Some topping ingredients, like anchovies, olives, capers and many cheeses, are already very salty. You may, in some cases, wish to omit the salt entirely and substitute one of the flavorings listed below.

Flavorings

Pizza dough may be flavored with herbs, spices or other flavoring ingredients. Add them to the dough after it has risen and doubled in bulk. Knead briefly to insure even distribution and proceed with recipe.

Freshly Ground Black Pepper. This adds piquancy and bite to pizza dough. Use 1 tablespoon or more, to taste. (Do not substitute pre-ground black pepper because it will have little flavor or aroma.)

Rosemary. Add 1 to 2 teaspoons finely minced fresh rosemary or half the amount dried rosemary.

Sage. Add 1 teaspoon finely minced fresh sage or ½ teaspoon crumbled dried sage.

Thyme. Add ½ to 1 teaspoon finely minced fresh thyme or crumbled dried thyme.

Bacon. Add ¼ cup crumbled crisply fried bacon.

Toppings

Inventing exciting and delicious toppings for pizza is a wonderful challenge for the creative cook. The guidelines and recipes that follow should be thought of as merely a starting point in the creation of your own pizza repertory. Once you have developed a feel for the sort of toppings you find most appealing, then freshness, excellence and availability of ingredients should be your guide. The selection of topping ingredients and their preparation, combination and arrangement is what will make your pizza unique.

The topping with which we are most familiar consists of a layer of tomato sauce that is covered with cheese and sprinkled with herbs and seasonings. Any number of other ingredients may be added: vegetables, hams, sausages, olives, anchovies, tuna, shellfish of almost every variety and other kinds of cheese.

Pizza Sauce. Use the recipe for basic pizza sauce that follows, or consider any of the tomato sauces in the Pasta section, Volume 4.

Cheese. Cheese used for pizza toppings may be divided into two basic categories—soft, melting cheeses and dry, grating cheeses.

Melting Cheese: In Italy, mozzarella made from the milk of the water buffalo is the cheese of choice for pizza toppings because it melts perfectly without acquiring a rubbery texture. Buffalo milk mozzarella is still very hard to find in this country, but you may be able to buy freshly made mozzarella in Italian neighborhoods and specialty stores. For those counting calories, skim milk mozzarella is the ideal choice.

Although mozzarella is the most commonly used melting cheese for a pizza topping, many other cheeses may be considered for a variety of flavors and textures. Other such cheeses suitable for pizza toppings are Fontina, Jack, bel paese and Gruyère.

In a category by themselves, because they do not melt in the same way but add a delicious taste and texture all their own, are goat cheeses such as the many varieties of chèvre now so popular.

• Grating Cheese: The thing to remember about grating cheeses, such as Parmesan, Romano and asiago, is that a little goes a long way. They are usually sharp-tasting and add a special tang to pizza toppings. Dry cheeses are best grated just before use so that they do not dry out.

Tomatoes. The ideal tomato for a pizza topping is a vine-ripened Italian plum tomato, with the skin and seeds removed. As these are nearly impossible to find unless you grow them yourself, the next best choice is good-quality imported Italian plum tomatoes. In season, fresh ripe tomatoes may also be used but all the juice must

4

Basic Pizza Dough

one 12-inch round
or 9×13-inch oblong pizza

1¼	teaspoons active dry yeast
½	cup warm water (110° to 115°F)
1½	cups unbleached all-purpose flour
1	teaspoon salt
1	tablespoon olive oil

Note: The inside of an unlit gas oven with a pilot light is a perfect place to let the dough rise. For a longer, slower rising, keep in a cool place (60° to 70°F) or even in the refrigerator for a few hours or overnight.

1 Sprinkle yeast over warm water and stir to dissolve. If you are unsure whether your yeast is active, proof it (see Volume 7 Index).

2 Sift flour and salt into medium-size mixing bowl. Make hollow in center and pour in dissolved yeast and olive oil.

3 Stir the flour into liquid with a wooden spoon until dough holds together.

OR Pour the warm water and yeast into bowl of food processor fitted with the metal blade. Pulse to dissolve.

AND Add flour, salt and olive oil and process till dough forms a ball.

4 Remove dough to a lightly floured work area and knead for 10 minutes, or until dough is smooth and elastic.

5 Shape dough into a ball and place in lightly oiled mixing bowl. Turn several times to coat.

6 Cover bowl with plastic wrap and put in warm draft-free place to rise for about 3 hours, or until dough has doubled in bulk.

Pizza with Anchovies and Olives

one 12-inch round
or 9×13-inch oblong pizza

2	tablespoons olive oil
1	can (28 ounces) Italian plum tomatoes, drained and cut into small pieces
¼	teaspoon sugar
	freshly ground pepper
1	teaspoon dried orégano
1	recipe risen pizza dough
8	ounces mozzarella cheese
1	can (2 ounces) flat anchovy fillets, drained
12	small pitted black olives

1 Preheat oven to 450°F. Heat oil in saucepan; add tomatoes, sugar, pepper to taste and orégano. Simmer, stirring occasionally, for 10 minutes. Remove from heat. Let cool.

2 Punch down risen dough and knead briefly. Shape into a ball. Brush baking sheet with oil.

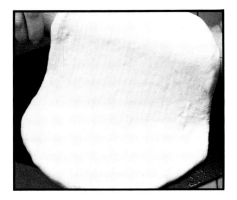

3 Roll dough out into a 12-inch circle or a 9 × 13-inch oblong. Drape it over rolling pin and transfer to baking sheet.

4 Press outer edge of dough upward with fingertips to make a slight rim.

5 Spread tomato sauce over pizza. Cut cheese into thin slices and arrange over the top.

6 Arrange anchovies in a lattice pattern over the cheese.

7 Place an olive inside each lattice "diamond."

8 Bake for 15 to 20 minutes, or until cheese has melted and edges of the dough have turned brown.

Aunt Veronica's American Pan Pizza

This pizza is simplicity itself. It is made in an unconventional way and can be ready to serve in less than 30 minutes. Unlike a traditional pizza made with a yeast dough, this pizza is made with flour, baking powder and oil, and is fried rather than baked.

6 portions

Dough

1½	cups unbleached all-purpose flour
1	tablespoon baking powder
½	teaspoon salt
4	to 5 tablespoons olive oil

Topping

1	can (14 ounces) Italian plum tomatoes
6	ounces Cheddar cheese
1½	teaspoons minced garlic, or 1 teaspoon garlic powder
1½	teaspoons dried orégano
1	can (2 ounces) flat anchovy fillets
10	pimiento-stuffed green olives

1 Sift dry ingredients into a bowl and make a well in the center.

2 Pour in 2 tablespoons oil and 3 to 4 tablespoons cold water. Mix together to make a soft dough.

3 Turn dough out on a floured board and knead lightly until smooth and free from cracks.

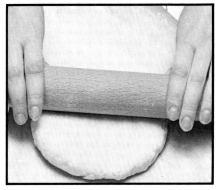

4 Heat remaining oil, enough to cover base of a large frying pan. Roll out dough to size of frying pan.

5 Transfer dough to frying pan and fry over low heat for about 5 minutes, until lightly browned.

6 Turn dough over and fry for an additional 5 minutes, adding more oil if necessary. Preheat broiler.

7 Drain the tomatoes and grate the cheese. Spread the tomatoes over dough in pan and distribute cheese over top.

8 Sprinkle cheese with minced garlic or garlic powder and herbs. Drain the anchovies and arrange in a lattice design over cheese.

9 Place a stuffed olive in each lattice "diamond." Put pan under broiler about 4 inches from heat until cheese melts and begins to brown.

10 Slide pizza onto a large warmed plate and cut into 6 portions to serve.

be removed along with the seeds and skin or the topping will be too watery.

Other Vegetables. Many other vegetables can be used as a topping for pizza but they should be of the highest quality and as fresh as possible. They are usually sautéed or steamed before being used.

Meats and Seafood. Pepperoni and fresh Italian sausage are the meats most commonly used for pizza toppings, but there are many other delicious possibilities. Use your imagination and consider the sausages and cured meats that are available in your area. Prosciutto, chorizo, kielbasa and homemade country-style sausage are all excellent toppings for pizza. Anchovies, clams, mussels, shrimps and oysters are only some of the many seafood toppings that can appear on pizzas.

Equipment

The Oven. Although a recipe for fried pizza appears in the preceeding pages, pizzas are traditionally baked in an oven, and your oven is the single most important piece of equipment in pizza making. The best pizzas are baked quickly at very high temperatures. Restaurants and bakeries that specialize in making pizza are equipped with ovens that reach very high temperatures (600° to 700°F) and purists maintain that authentic pizzas can be made only in wood-burning ovens that can reach temperatures of 800°F. It is true that a brick-lined wood-burning oven can produce superlative pizzas with very crisp crusts and an overall smoky tang, but there is no reason why you cannot make very good pizza in your home oven if it can reach a temperature of at least 450°F. A gas oven is preferable to an electric one, although electric ovens can work perfectly well as long as they do not have a built-in thermostat, which turns the oven off when it gets as hot as you need it and doesn't maintain the highest heat.

Tiles and Baking Stones. The floor of a regular oven may be lined with unglazed quarry tiles to approximate the direct, intense heat of a wood-burning oven. The oven is preheated for a minimum of 30 minutes (an hour is even better) and the pizza is placed directly on the hot tiles.

Specially designed baking stones are available in many cookware shops throughout the country and these are excellent as well, though the pizza doesn't slide onto them as easily as it does onto quarry tiles. Baking stones must also be preheated for a minimum of 30 minutes.

Pizza Paddle. If you use quarry tiles or baking stones, a wooden pizza paddle, called a peel, is the most impressive and professional way to slide an unbaked pizza onto them. The paddle is sprinkled with corn meal to prevent the unbaked dough from sticking and the pizza is assembled directly on the paddle. Then with a quick slide and a jerk of the wrist the pizza is deposited on the hot baking surface. To remove the pizza when it is done, lift the edges with a spatula and slide the paddle underneath. If you make a lot of pizzas you may wish to invest in this dandy accouterment of the pizza maker's craft, but it is neither inexpensive nor unobtrusive. A large wooden paddle in a small-size kitchen may in fact present more problems than it solves. So be inventive. Any light, hard, thin board can substitute for a paddle, or in a pinch, the back side of a baking sheet or jelly roll pan will do the trick.

Baking Sheets and Pans. Any large, heavy baking sheet or jelly roll pan can be used to make pizza. Brush the surface lightly with vegetable oil. Arrange your pizza dough, cover with topping and place in the oven.

Pizza Cutter. A specially designed wheeled cutter will add a note of professional pizzazz when you are serving your home-baked pie. It is inexpensive and can cut through layers of gooey cheese with miraculous ease.

Making Pizza

To make the dough, begin by dissolving the yeast in warm (110° to 115°F) water. Then mix and knead the dough by hand or in a food processor.

Once the dough has been kneaded to the proper consistency it is set to rise in a warm place for approximately 3 hours, or until it is doubled in size. The cook is given a great deal of leeway at this stage because the rising can be slowed down to fit almost any schedule. Once risen, the dough may stand for an extra hour or so without any impairment, or it may be refrigerated for as long as 24 hours. In fact, many people think that dough given a long, slow rise in a cool place develops better flavor. After the dough has risen to double its original volume, it can be frozen with no loss of flavor or texture. Simply punch it down and wrap in several layers of plastic wrap. It can remain in the freezer for as long as two months. Let frozen dough thaw for several hours at room temperature or overnight in the refrigerator before rolling it out and shaping it for pizza.

Pizza dough undergoes only one rising before it is baked. Only focaccia, a breadlike cousin of the pizza, is set to rise a second time after it has received its savory toppings. The main difference is that with regular pizza the crust serves as a thin vehicle for the various toppings; with focaccia, the thin topping is there to offset the thick, rich crusty bread that is the basis.

Prepare topping ingredients while dough is rising. Precook all ingredients that require it, drain well to prevent pizza from becoming soggy, and let cool to lukewarm before spreading on the dough.

Rolling Out the Dough. It takes years of practice to acquire the skills of a *pizzaiolo* (pizza maker), who stretches the pizza dough while twirling it in the air. In the meantime you can achieve satisfying results with a rolling pin.

Punch down the risen dough, remove to a floured board, and knead briefly. If you are adding any flavorings to the dough, do it now. Roll out the dough into a circle or oblong to a thickness of about 1/4 inch, then use your fingers to press the dough out from the center so that the rim is slightly thicker than the center. Place in an oiled baking pan, on a baking sheet, or on a pizza paddle that has been dusted with corn meal. Arrange the topping of your choice in an attractive pattern and bake for the specified time.

Pizza with Mushrooms and Red Peppers

one 12-inch round or 9 × 13-inch oblong pizza

1	small onion	¼	teaspoon salt
2	garlic cloves		freshly ground pepper
4	ounces mushrooms	1	red bell pepper
1½	cups Italian plum tomatoes, drained	8	ounces mozzarella cheese
1	tablespoon olive oil	1	recipe risen pizza dough
		1	teaspoon dried orégano

Preheat oven to 450°F. Peel the onion and garlic and chop. Wipe the mushrooms clean with a damp cloth or paper towel and slice thin. Cut the tomatoes into small pieces. Heat the olive oil in a saucepan over moderate heat, add the onions and garlic, and cook for 5 minutes, or until slightly softened. Add the mushrooms and sauté, stirring occasionally, for 3 minutes, or until they are tender. Add the salt and pepper to taste. Remove from heat and set aside. Cut the red pepper in half, core, seed, and cut into very thin slices. Cut the mozzarella into very thin slices or shred in a food processor or on a grater.

Punch down the risen dough and remove to a lightly floured work surface. Knead it briefly and shape into a ball. Roll out the dough to a 12-inch circle or a 9 × 13-inch oblong. Brush a baking sheet lightly with vegetable oil or sprinkle a pizza paddle with corn meal. Transfer the pizza dough onto the baking sheet or paddle. Pinch outer edge of dough and push up to form a slight rim. Arrange the chopped tomatoes over the pizza dough. Sprinkle with orégano and salt and pepper to taste. Cover with red pepper strips, mushrooms, onion and garlic and top with mozzarella slices.

Bake the pizza for 15 to 20 minutes, or until sides are puffy and golden brown and the topping is bubbling.

Whole-Wheat Pizza Dough

In this dough part of the all-purpose white flour is re-placed with whole-wheat flour for a chewier, more nutty- *flavored pizza crust. It will not be as crisp as a crust made with white flour.*

one 12-inch round or 9 × 13-inch oblong pizza

1¼ teaspoons active dry yeast	¾ cup whole-wheat flour
½ cup warm water (110° to 115°F)	1 teaspoon salt
¾ cup unbleached all-purpose flour	1 tablespoon olive oil

Follow instructions for Basic Pizza Dough.

Semolina Pizza Dough

Pizza dough made with semolina flour is a little harder to work because it is much less elastic, but it makes the crispiest pizza crust of all.

one 12-inch round or 9 × 13-inch oblong pizza

Substitute 1½ cups semolina flour for the unbleached all-purpose flour in the recipe for Basic Pizza Dough. The dough will take longer to rise.

Basic Pizza Sauce

makes about 2 cups

1 can (28 ounces) Italian plum tomatoes	¼ teaspoon sugar
3 garlic cloves	½ teaspoon freshly ground pepper
¼ cup olive oil	1 tablespoon chopped fresh basil or orégano, or 1½ teaspoons dried orégano
1 teaspoon salt	

Drain the tomatoes and reserve the juice for another pur-pose. Cut tomatoes into small pieces. Peel the garlic and chop it fine. Heat the oil in a heavy saucepan and add the tomatoes, garlic, salt, sugar, pepper and herbs. Reduce heat to low and simmer the sauce, stirring occasionally, for 15 to 20 minutes, or until it is thick and smooth.

Note: This sauce can be used in place of any of the other tomato-based sauces called for in the following recipes. It keeps in the refrigerator for up to a week and may be frozen for several months. You will need about 1 cup of sauce for a 12-inch round pizza pie, so if you are freezing it you may want to package the sauce in 1-cup containers.

Asparagus Pizza

You may adapt this recipe to any vegetable in season.

one 12-inch round or 9 × 13-inch oblong pizza

1 pound small to medium-size asparagus	12 ounces mozzarella cheese
	1 recipe risen pizza dough

Preheat oven to 450°F. Trim the tough stems from the asparagus and peel the stalks up to ½ inch from the tips. Plunge into boiling water for 1 to 2 minutes, depending on size, then drain, and refresh under cold running water. Cut the mozzarella into very thin slices.

Punch down the risen dough and remove to a lightly

floured work surface. Knead it briefly and shape into a ball. Roll out the dough to a 12-inch circle or a 9 × 13-inch oblong. Brush a baking sheet lightly with vegetable oil or sprinkle a pizza paddle with corn meal. Transfer the pizza dough onto the baking sheet or paddle. Pinch outer edge of dough and push up to form a slight rim. Arrange half the cheese over the pizza dough. Arrange the asparagus like spokes of a wheel on top and cover with remaining cheese.

Bake the pizza for 15 to 20 minutes, or until sides are puffy and golden brown and the topping is bubbling.

Four Seasons Pizza

one 12-inch round or 9 × 13-inch oblong pizza

½	pound fresh ripe tomatoes or 1½ cups canned Italian plum tomatoes, drained
¼	pound mushrooms
1	tablespoon unsalted butter
1	can (7 ounces) tuna fish
¼	pound sliced salami
2	ounces Edam cheese
1	recipe risen pizza dough
1	teaspoon dried orégano

Preheat oven to 450°F. If using fresh tomatoes, bring a saucepan of water to a boil and off heat immerse the tomatoes for 60 seconds. Refresh under cold running water. When cool enough to handle, peel off the skins. Cut tomatoes into thin slices and let drain in a colander. Wipe the mushrooms with a damp cloth or paper towels and cut into thin slices. Place butter in a small skillet and set over medium heat until melted. Add the mushrooms and sauté over medium heat until lightly browned. Drain the tuna fish and break into small pieces with a fork. Remove skin from salami and cut each slice into quarters. Grate the cheese into a small bowl; you should have about ½ cup.

Punch down the risen pizza dough and remove it to a lightly floured work surface. Knead it briefly and shape into a ball. Roll out the dough to a 12-inch circle or a 9 × 13-inch oblong. Brush a baking sheet lightly with vegetable oil or sprinkle a pizza paddle with corn meal. Transfer the pizza dough to the baking sheet or paddle. Pinch outer edge of dough to form a slight rim.

Mark the top of the dough into four equal quarters with a round-bladed knife. Arrange tomato slices on one quarter of the dough, the mushrooms on another quarter, the tuna on the third quarter, and the salami on the last quarter. Sprinkle the cheese over the entire surface of the pizza and sprinkle the orégano over the cheese.

Bake the pizza for 15 to 20 minutes, or until the sides are puffy and golden brown and the topping is bubbling.

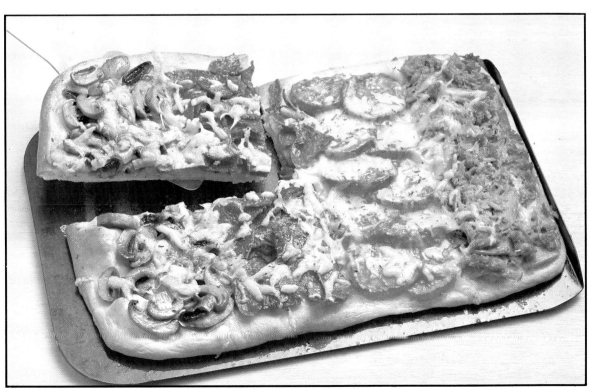

Pizza Capri

Pizza with capers and artichoke hearts.

one 12-inch round or 9 × 13-inch oblong pizza

1	small onion	½	teaspoon salt
1	garlic clove		freshly ground pepper
1½	cups canned Italian plum tomatoes, drained	8	ounces mozzarella cheese
1	tablespoon olive oil	6	pitted black olives
½	teaspoon dried marjoram	1	recipe risen pizza dough
½	teaspoon dried orégano	2	to 3 teaspoons capers
		1	jar (6 ounces) artichoke hearts

Preheat oven to 450°F. Peel and mince the onion and the garlic. Cut the tomatoes into small pieces. Heat the olive oil in a saucepan set over moderate heat. Add the onion and garlic and cook, stirring occasionally, for 5 minutes, or until slightly softened. Add the tomatoes, herbs, salt, and pepper to taste. Simmer gently for 5 minutes, until sauce has thickened slightly. Remove from the heat and set aside. Cut the mozzarella into very thin slices and cut the olives in half lengthwise.

Punch down the risen dough and remove to a lightly floured work surface. Knead it briefly and shape into a ball.

Roll out the dough to a 12-inch circle or a 9 × 13-inch oblong. Brush a baking sheet lightly with vegetable oil or sprinkle a pizza paddle with corn meal. Transfer the pizza dough to the baking sheet or paddle. Pinch outer edge of dough and push up to form a slight rim. Spread tomato sauce evenly over the pizza dough, cover with mozzarella slices and arrange olives, capers and artichoke hearts over all.

Bake the pizza for 15 to 20 minutes, until sides are puffy and golden brown and the topping is bubbling.

Pizza alla Margherita

Simply tomatoes, cheese and herbs, and simply delicious.

one 12-inch round or 9 × 13-inch oblong pizza

1	pound ripe tomatoes or 1½ cups canned Italian plum tomatoes, drained			freshly ground pepper
2	tablespoons olive oil		1	recipe risen pizza dough
1	garlic clove		8	ounces mozzarella cheese
¼	teaspoon sugar		¾	ounce Parmesan cheese
½	teaspoon salt		1	tablespoon chopped fresh basil, orégano or parsley

Preheat oven to 450°F. If using fresh tomatoes, bring a saucepan of water to a boil and, off heat, immerse tomatoes for 60 seconds. Refresh under cold running water and when cool enough to handle peel away skins. Seed the tomatoes and chop into small pieces. If using canned tomatoes, chop into small pieces. Heat the olive oil in a saucepan and add the tomatoes. Peel and mince the garlic clove and add to the tomatoes. Add sugar, salt, and pepper to taste. Cook for 10 minutes over medium heat.

Punch down the risen dough and remove to a lightly floured work surface. Knead it briefly and shape into a ball. Roll out the dough to a 12-inch circle or a 9 × 13-inch oblong. Brush a baking sheet lightly with vegetable oil or sprinkle a pizza paddle with corn meal. Transfer the pizza dough to the baking sheet or paddle. Pinch outer edge of dough and push up to form a slight rim.

Cut the mozzarella into very thin slices or shred in a food processor or on a grater. Grate the Parmesan cheese; you should have 3 tablespoons. Spread the mozzarella over the pizza dough. Cover with a layer of tomato sauce. Sprinkle with Parmesan cheese and the chopped herbs.

Bake the pizza for 15 to 20 minutes, or until sides are puffy and golden brown and the topping is bubbling.

Pizza with Eggplant and Tomatoes

one 12-inch round or 9 × 13-inch oblong pizza

1	medium-size eggplant, about 1 pound		1	teaspoon dried orégano
½	cup olive oil		½	teaspoon salt
1	medium-size onion			freshly ground pepper
1	garlic clove		2	ounces Parmesan cheese
1½	cups canned Italian plum tomatoes, drained		8	ounces mozzarella cheese
			1	recipe risen pizza dough

Preheat oven to 450°F. Peel the eggplant and cut into ¼-inch rounds. Reserve 1 tablespoon of the olive oil and heat the remainder in a heavy frying pan. When the oil is hot, fry the eggplant over moderate heat for 2 to 3 minutes on each side, or just until the eggplant slices are tender and browned. Drain cooked eggplant slices on paper towels.

Peel and slice the onion, peel and chop the garlic, and cut the tomatoes into small pieces. Heat the remaining table-spoon of olive oil in a saucepan over moderate heat. Add the garlic and onion and cook, stirring occasionally, for 5 minutes. Add the tomatoes, orégano, salt, and pepper to taste. Simmer gently for about 10 minutes, or until the sauce has thickened slightly. Remove from the heat and set aside. Grate the Parmesan cheese; you should have ½ cup. Cut the mozzarella into very thin slices or shred in a food processor or on a grater.

Punch down the risen dough and remove to a lightly floured work surface. Knead it briefly and shape into a ball. Roll out the dough to a 12-inch circle or a 9 × 13-inch oblong. Brush a baking sheet lightly with vegetable oil or sprinkle a pizza paddle with corn meal. Transfer the pizza dough to the baking sheet or paddle. Pinch outer edge of dough and push up to form a slight rim. Spread tomato sauce evenly on the pizza dough. Lay the eggplant slices over the tomato sauce. Sprinkle with the Parmesan and arrange mozzarella slices on top.

Bake the pizza for 25 to 30 minutes, or until sides are puffy and golden brown and the topping is bubbling.
Variation: For a less fattening topping, brush the eggplant slices lightly with olive oil, arrange them in a single layer on a baking sheet, and bake in a 400°F oven for 15 to 20 minutes, or just until eggplant slices are tender.

14

Pepperoni Pizza

one 12-inch round or 9 × 13-inch oblong pizza

1 small onion	½ teaspoon dried basil
1 garlic clove	½ teaspoon dried orégano
1½ cups canned plum tomatoes, drained	1 bay leaf
3 tablespoons olive oil	8 ounces mozzarella cheese
½ teaspoon salt	1 pound pepperoni sausage
freshly ground pepper	1 recipe risen pizza dough
	1 tablespoon chopped fresh parsley

Preheat oven to 450°F. Peel the onion and slice it. Peel and chop the garlic. Cut the tomatoes into small pieces. Heat 2 tablespoons of the olive oil in a saucepan over moderate heat. Add the onion and garlic and sauté, stirring occasionally, for 5 to 7 minutes, or until the onion is soft and translucent. Add the tomatoes, salt, pepper to taste, basil, orégano and bay leaf. Simmer for 10 minutes, or until the sauce thickens slightly. Remove from heat and set aside.

Cut the mozzarella into thin slices or shred in a food processor or on a grater. Cut the pepperoni into very thin slices.

Punch down the risen dough and remove to a lightly floured work surface. Knead it briefly and shape into a ball. Roll out the dough to a 12-inch circle or a 9 × 13-inch oblong. Brush a baking sheet lightly with vegetable oil or sprinkle a pizza paddle with corn meal. Transfer the pizza dough to the baking sheet or paddle. Pinch outer edge of dough and push up to form a slight rim. Spread tomato sauce over the pizza dough. Arrange mozzarella slices on top, sprinkle with parsley, and arrange pepperoni slices over all. Drizzle with the remaining tablespoon of olive oil.

Bake the pizza for 15 to 20 minutes, or until sides are puffy and golden brown and the topping is bubbling.

Variation: Arrange the pepperoni slices as the first layer. Cover with tomato sauce, and end with cheese, herbs and oil. This keeps the pepperoni from drying out and provides an element of surprise as well.

Pizzetine

These miniature pizzas make mouth-watering and impressive canapés or light snacks. You can substitute bay scallops or shelled Little Neck clams for the shrimps, or even sausage or chunks of ham.

ten 3½-inch round mini pizzas

20	medium-size shrimps, about ¾ pound		1	can (14 ounces) Italian plum tomatoes
2	garlic cloves		1	tablespoon tomato paste
4	scallions		¼	teaspoon sugar
10	pimiento-stuffed green olives		½	teaspoon salt
4	tablespoons olive oil			freshly ground pepper
2	tablespoons chopped parsley		1	recipe risen pizza dough

Preheat oven to 450°F. Shell and devein the shrimps. Peel the garlic and mince. Trim scallions, separate the white part from the green, and mince all the white. Mince enough of the green to measure 2 tablespoons. Mince the stuffed olives. Place the shrimps, 2 tablespoons of the olive oil, half of the minced garlic, the green part of scallions, chopped olives and chopped parsley in a bowl and toss well. Cover and set aside but do not refrigerate.

Heat the remaining 2 tablespoons of olive oil in a saucepan. Add the minced scallion white and remaining garlic to the oil and cook gently over medium-low heat for about 5 minutes, or until soft. Stir frequently. Add the shrimps and sauté 2 to 3 minutes or just until they turn an orangey-pink. Remove from the oil and reserve. Drain the tomatoes and cut them into small pieces. Add them to the saucepan along with the tomato paste, sugar, salt, and pepper to taste. Cook over moderate heat for 15 to 20 minutes, until the sauce has reduced and thickened. Remove from the heat and set aside. Brush a large baking sheet with vegetable oil.

Punch down the risen dough and remove to a lightly floured work surface. Knead it briefly and shape into a ball. Roll it out to a large rectangle and cut out 3½-inch rounds with a cookie cutter. Lightly knead the trimmings together, roll out again, and cut out more rounds until you have 10.

Allow the rounds to rest for a few minutes. They will shrink a little so before proceeding gently stretch them back to their original size. Place as many as will fit on the prepared baking sheet, leaving 2 inches of space between each one. You may have to cook them in two batches; keep the dough covered if it has to wait.

Place a tablespoonful of tomato sauce on each round of dough and spread out evenly to the edges. Bake for 12 minutes and remove from oven. Distribute the reserved shrimps and chopped herbs evenly on the pizzas and return to the oven for 4 to 5 minutes more, or until the shrimps are warm and the crust is lightly browned.

Pizza with Prosciutto

one 12-inch round or 9 × 13-inch oblong pizza

1½	cups canned Italian plum tomatoes, drained		2	tablespoons chopped fresh basil, or 1 teaspoon dried orégano
6	ounces Fontina cheese			freshly ground pepper
4	ounces prosciutto, in one piece		1	teaspoon olive oil
1	recipe risen pizza dough			

Preheat oven to 450°F. Chop the tomatoes into small pieces; cut the Fontina into thin slices; and cut the prosciutto into matchstick strips.

Punch down the risen dough and remove to a lightly floured work surface. Knead it briefly and shape into a ball. Roll out the dough to a 12-inch circle or a 9 × 13-inch oblong. Brush a baking sheet lightly with vegetable oil or sprinkle a pizza paddle with corn meal. Transfer the pizza

dough to the baking sheet or paddle. Pinch outer edge of dough and push up to form a slight rim. Arrange the chopped tomatoes over the pizza dough. Sprinkle with fresh basil or dried orégano and freshly ground pepper to taste. Arrange slices of Fontina on top and strew with prosciutto strips. Sprinkle with the olive oil.

Bake the pizza for 15 to 20 minutes, or until the sides are puffy and golden brown and the topping is bubbling.

Basic Focaccia Dough

Long before pizza there was focaccia—a chewy, yeasty, crusty bread flavored with any number of simple herbs and seasonings, for example, rosemary, sage, garlic, onion, coarse salt, coarsely ground pepper. Sometimes more substantial additions are made, such as chopped prosciutto. The focaccia can also be split and filled. The dough for focaccia is quite similar to pizza dough, but it is usually saltier and enriched and flavored with olive oil. You may freely substitute any pizza dough recipe for the following focaccia dough. Focaccia may be baked in a 15-inch round pan or a 16-inch square pan, or directly on unglazed quarry tiles or on a baking stone.

one 15-inch round or 16-inch square focaccia

1	envelope (1 scant tablespoon) active dry yeast	3	cups unbleached all-purpose flour
1	cup warm water (110° to 115°F)	2	teaspoons salt
		¼	cup olive oil

Follow instructions for Basic Pizza Dough.

Garlic Focaccia

The original garlic bread, and still the best.

one 15-inch round or 16-inch square focaccia

4	large garlic cloves	1	teaspoon olive oil
1	recipe risen Basic Focaccia Dough or 1 doubled recipe risen pizza dough	1	teaspoon coarse salt

Peel the garlic cloves and cut them into tiny slivers. Punch down the risen dough and remove to a lightly floured work surface. Knead it briefly and press directly into an oiled 15-inch round pan or 16-inch square pan; or roll it into a circle and place on an oiled baking sheet or a pizza paddle that has been sprinkled with corn meal. Remember that focaccia is always much thicker than a pizza. Rub the surface with olive oil and stud it all over with the garlic slivers. Sprinkle with coarse salt. Cover with a towel and let rise for 30 minutes. While dough is rising, preheat oven to 450°F.

Bake focaccia for 15 to 20 minutes, or until sides are puffy and golden brown.

Variations: Omit the garlic and use only salt and olive oil. Add a generous grinding of pepper.

Add 1 teaspoon of fresh rosemary needles or leave out garlic and use only rosemary.

Slice an onion very thin and spread it over the dough. Brush the onion with a tablespoon of olive oil before baking. Add salt and pepper to taste.

Pissaladière

These savory pizzalike tartlets hail from Provence, where they are eaten at any time of day or night as a traditional and delicious snack. Although best eaten hot, they may be served lukewarm or even at room temperature. You can also make the pissaladière as a round 12-inch pie.

9 tartlets

Pastry

2	cups unbleached all-purpose flour	4	tablespoons unsalted butter
½	teaspoon salt	¼	cup vegetable shortening
		3	to 4 tablespoons ice water

Filling

6	medium-size onions	¼	cup olive oil
2	garlic cloves		freshly ground pepper
3	large ripe tomatoes, or 1½ cups canned Italian plum tomatoes, drained	1	can (2 ounces) flat anchovy fillets, drained
		27	pitted black olives, preferably Niçoises

Make the pastry: Sift the flour and salt into a medium-size mixing bowl. Cut the butter into small pieces and add it and the vegetable shortening to the flour. Use two table knives or your fingertips to blend the flour and fats until the mixture resembles coarse meal. Mix in enough water to form the dough into a ball. Alternatively, place the flour and salt in the bowl of a food processor. Add the butter and vegetable shortening and pulse on and off several times to blend. With the motor on, add the water until dough forms a ball. Wrap dough in plastic wrap and refrigerate for 30 minutes.

For the filling, peel the onions and slice very thin. Peel the garlic and slice thin. If using fresh tomatoes, bring a saucepan of water to a boil. Submerge tomatoes, remove from heat, and leave for 1 minute. Peel tomatoes, seed, and chop fine. If using canned tomatoes, cut them into small pieces. Heat the olive oil in a large skillet. Add the onion and garlic and cook over low heat for about 30 minutes, or until very soft but not browned. Add the tomatoes and pepper to taste and cook for 45 minutes more over low heat, until the mixture is like a purée.

Preheat oven to 375°F. Brush nine fluted tartlet tins with oil and set aside. Roll out the dough to a large rectangle approximately ¾ inch thick. Cut out 9 circles of dough with a 4-inch round pastry cutter. Line tartlet tins with dough circles and crimp the edges. Prick dough all over with a fork. Bake the dough blind (see Volume 2, page 86): Press aluminum foil on top of the dough and fill with dried beans. Place the tins on a baking sheet and bake for 10 minutes.

Remove baking sheet from oven and remove the foil and beans. Return tartlet tins to the oven and bake for 5 minutes more, or until pastry is golden brown and baked through. While the pastry is baking, reheat the filling. Remove tart shells from the oven and let cool for 5 minutes. Then remove pastry cases from the tins and arrange on a serving platter.

Spoon the warm filling into the pastry cases. Arrange anchovy fillets in a lattice pattern across the top and dot with olives.

Variation: The same topping may be spread on regular unbaked pizza dough and baked like a pizza.

Calzone

This recipe for delicious, savory pizza turnovers calls for twice the amount of dough, so simply double all the ingredients, except for the salt, called for in the Basic Pizza Dough recipe.

4 calzoni

6	ounces prosciutto
6	ounces mozzarella cheese
1	egg
1	doubled recipe risen pizza dough

1	tablespoon minced fresh parsley
	freshly ground pepper
4	teaspoons olive oil

Preheat oven to 450°F. Cut prosciutto and mozzarella cheese into ¼-inch dice. Mix together and reserve. Beat the egg in a small bowl and reserve.

Punch down risen dough and remove to a lightly floured work surface. Knead it briefly, shape into a ball, and divide into four equal pieces. Roll each piece out into a circle approximately 6 inches in diameter. Brush the edge of one circle of dough with the beaten egg. Place one quarter of the ham and cheese mixture on one half of the dough circle. Sprinkle with parsley and freshly ground pepper to taste and drizzle with 1 teaspoon olive oil. Fold the dough circle over so that the filling is completely enclosed and press firmly around the edges to seal. Repeat procedure with the remaining dough circles.

Brush the surface of each calzone with the remaining beaten egg. With a fork, prick steam vents in the top of each calzone. Brush a baking sheet with oil and use a spatula to transfer each calzone to the sheet. Space the calzoni well apart to allow for expansion while they bake. Cover with a towel and let them relax for 15 minutes.

Bake the calzoni for 20 minutes, or until puffed and browned.

FILLING VARIATIONS:

Ricotta, Gorgonzola and Basil

4	ounces Gorgonzola cheese
12	ounces ricotta cheese
2	tablespoons chopped scallions

1	tablespoon finely chopped fresh basil

Crumble the Gorgonzola into small pieces and mix with the ricotta.

Add scallions and basil and mix well.

Broccoli, Garlic and Ricotta

1	bunch broccoli
½	slice bread
¼	cup olive oil

1	garlic clove
8	ounces ricotta cheese
	freshly ground pepper

Bring a large pot of water to a boil. Trim away tough ends of the broccoli and peel the stalks. Drop into boiling water and cook 5 minutes or until just tender. Drain and refresh under cold running water and cut into small pieces. Reduce the bread to crumbs in a food processor or blender. You should have about 2 tablespoons. Heat the oil in a skillet. Peel and chop the garlic and sauté in the oil until golden. Add the broccoli and cook 5 minutes. Add the bread crumbs and stir to combine; remove from heat. Let cool and mix with ricotta. Add freshly ground pepper to taste.

Goat Cheese and Prosciutto

4	ounces chèvre, imported or domestic or a mixture
6	ounces Fontina cheese
1	slice prosciutto, about ½ inch thick

2	tablespoons finely minced parsley
	freshly ground pepper

Crumble the chèvre, shred the Fontina, and cut prosciutto into fine dice. Combine all ingredients, until well blended, adding pepper to taste.

Pizza with Four Cheeses

*An all-white pizza, and very elegant indeed. Don't hesi-
tate to be creative and substitute any other cheeses of
your choice.*

one 12-inch round or 9 × 13-inch oblong pizza

1 ounce Parmesan cheese	8 ounces mozzarella cheese
1 ounce Romano cheese	2 tablespoons chopped fresh parsley
1 egg	freshly ground pepper
8 ounces ricotta cheese	1 recipe risen pizza dough

Preheat oven to 450°F. Grate the Parmesan and Romano. You should have about ¼ cup of each. Break the egg into a medium-size mixing bowl and beat it lightly. Add the ricotta, Parmesan and Romano. Cut the mozzarella into very small pieces or shred it in a food processor or on a grater. Add it to the mixture along with the parsley and freshly ground pepper to taste. Mix well and taste for seasoning.

Punch down the risen dough and remove to a lightly floured work surface. Knead it briefly and shape into a ball. Roll out the dough to a 12-inch circle or a 9 × 13-inch oblong. Brush a baking sheet lightly with vegetable oil or

sprinkle a pizza paddle with corn meal. Transfer the pizza dough to the baking sheet or paddle. Pinch outer edge of dough and push up to form a slight rim. Spread the cheese mixture evenly to within an inch of the edges of the pizza dough. Pull the edges up and over slightly to prevent melted cheese from oozing out.

Bake for 25 to 30 minutes, or until sides are puffy and golden brown and the topping is bubbling.
Variation: For a touch of sheer luxury, use a vegetable peeler to slice a fresh white truffle over the surface of the pizza the minute it emerges from the oven.

Quattrostagione Pizza

(Pizza with Four Toppings)

6 individual pizzas

1	recipe risen pizza dough	3	tablespoons olive oil

Base Topping

8	ounces Cheddar cheese	2	ounces Parmesan cheese

Tomato Topping

1	pound tomatoes	6	anchovy fillets
1	teaspoon dried basil	24	pitted black olives

Artichoke Topping

6	slices prosciutto	6	ounces canned artichoke hearts

Shrimp Topping

6	ounces mozzarella cheese	¼	teaspoon salt
6	ounces shrimps	¼	teaspoon freshly ground pepper
8	ounces asparagus		

Mushroom and Pepperoni Topping

4	ounces mushrooms	6	ounces pepperoni sausage
2	tablespoons butter	¼	teaspoon paprika

Grate the Cheddar and Parmesan cheese for the base topping. Make the tomato topping. Drop the tomatoes in boiling water to cover, remove from the heat and leave for 60 seconds. Drain the tomatoes, run cold water over them, peel and halve. Squeeze gently to remove the seeds. Chop the tomatoes. Halve the pitted olives. To make the artichoke topping, halve the slices of prosciutto. Drain the artichoke hearts and cut into slices. Slice the mozzarella cheese for the shrimp topping. Shell the shrimps. Cut the tips from the asparagus, reserving the rest of the stalk for a soup or an omelet filling. Wash the tips thoroughly and steam until barely tender, about 2 minutes. Refresh the tips under cold running water, drain and, depending on their size, cut each tip into 3 or 4 pieces. Prepare the mushroom topping. Using a damp cloth or paper towel, wipe the mushrooms clean. Pare any brown bits from the stems. Slice the mushrooms. Melt the butter in a skillet and toss the mushrooms over medium-high heat for 3 minutes. Cut the pepperoni into ¾-inch lengths.

Preheat the oven to 450°F. Oil three large baking sheets with half the oil, and set them aside. Turn the risen dough onto a floured surface and knead it for 5 minutes. Divide the dough into seven equal-sized pieces, and roll each into a ball. Set one piece aside, and roll each of the remaining pieces of dough into a circle about ¼ inch thick. Place two of the dough circles on each of the baking sheets, leaving space between them.

Sprinkle the top of each pizza with the grated Cheddar and Parmesan cheese, and set the pizzas aside. Roll out the remaining piece of dough to a rectangle and cut it lengthwise into long strips, each about ¼ inch wide and 8 inches long. Use these strips to divide each pizza into quarters. Top one quarter of each pizza at a time. Start with the tomato topping, spooning the tomatoes onto one section of the pizza, then sprinkling them with the basil and laying on the anchovy fillets and halved olives. Top the second quarter with the prosciutto and sliced artichoke hearts. Lay overlapping slices of mozzarella on the third quarter, and cover the cheese with the shrimps and the asparagus tips. Sprinkle with the salt and pepper. Place the mushrooms and the pepperoni sausage on the fourth quarter, and sprinkle with the paprika.

Sprinkle the remaining olive oil over the pizza. Place the

pizzas in the oven, and bake for 15 to 20 minutes, or until the dough is crusty and the cheese has melted.

Remove the baking sheets from the oven. Transfer the pizzas to individual dishes and serve immediately.

Part Two

DEEP-FRYING MEAT, POULTRY AND FISH

"Along the side streets [of Seville] you will see stands where fish is fried and sold. . . . Go and watch the man in the first stand you pass. Behind him is a deep vat of hot oil, beside him the prepared flour, in front of him a wide variety of raw fish. Ask him for a mixed order, and he will dip the bright pink mullets, sole, fresh sardines and other fish into the flour and then gently slide them into the glittering oil. If you are a man he will tell you jokes, if a woman he will pay you compliments in the Andalusian accent of thick sibilants and shortened words, and he will know when the fish is done behind him and scoop it out, allowing it to drain while he prepares a cone of brown paper to hold it. . . . The fish, no matter what kind, will be so crisp that you must hold a hand under your mouth to catch the splintered slivers as you bite."

Peter S. Feibleman
The Cooking of Spain and Portugal

There is no doubt about it. Frying, one of the most common methods of cooking, is also one of the most highly suspect. These facts are not unrelated since America's ubiquitous fast-food restaurants daily serve up millions of pieces of greasy, indigestible, overcooked food that fairly reeks of rancid, overused oil. The result is empty calories, unnecessary cholesterol, heartburn and, of course, a bad reputation for fried foods— all quite needless. No one would recommend a steady diet composed exclusively of fried food, but done properly, with good fresh oil, frying adds scant amounts of fat to food and is one of the most delicious methods of cooking in the world.

Indeed, it comes as no surprise that frying is an honored technique of nearly every cuisine, distinguished in most cases by the frying medium most commonly employed. The French, of course, are partial to butter, which, though inappropriate for deep-frying, is perfect for the gentler

French method of sautéing. The Chinese use peanut oil for deep-frying as well as for their native specialty, stir-frying. In Germany it's goose fat; in Austria, lard. The Italians and Spanish, unsurprisingly, favor olive oil, and we in America lean toward vegetable oil or shortening, though bacon fat does yeoman duty here, too.

Almost any kind of food can be fried, but the method is most appropriate for relatively tender and moist meats or vegetables that do not need slow cooking or extra moisture to tenderize them. Then, too, deep-frying is best employed when the pieces to be cooked are fairly small, since the high cooking temperature required to seal in moisture would overcook larger pieces that needed longer cooking times.

The basic idea of frying, that is to say cooking food in hot oil or fat, is at least two thousand years old, and in that time at least three major and distinct techniques have evolved: panfrying, which requires the least amount of fat or oil—a mere film to keep the food from sticking to the pan; shallow frying, which employs an inch or less of oil; and deep-fat frying, which is the total immersion of food in hot oil—literally boiling in oil. Oddly enough, it is this last technique, the one that uses the greatest amount of oil, that results in food with the least oil added to it, at least when done properly. The reason is simply that the food, whether coated or not, is instantly sealed on all sides when lowered into the hot fat, so that as the cooking progresses no further fat is able to penetrate. Drained and served immediately, the result is a delight—crackling crisp on the outside, tender and juicy on the inside.

It is, in fact, the addition of a crisp texture to foods that gives frying much of its appeal. A coating, whether of flour, crumbs, batter, or any combination of these, enhances the crispness of the final product at the same time that it provides an even more effective seal that keeps moisture in and oil out. For this reason foods in the process of frying should be handled with great care so that the coating is not punctured.

Temperature is crucial in all forms of frying and should always be monitored carefully, with a thermometer whenever possible. Vegetable oils and vegetable shortenings have the highest tolerance for heat, and they add very little in the way of taste to the food that is fried in them.

Fried food is *not* "fast food." The very idea that it *can* be is responsible for most of the bad fried food in the world. But if greasy, soggy, badly fried food is the rule in certain quarters, there are other quarters in which perhaps a bit too much is made of the mystique of cooking good fried food. The careful choice of prime ingredients, the proper choice of oil, the right temperature, carefully maintained, and anyone can produce fried foods of the most heavenly lightness, flavor and texture.

DEEP-FRYING MEAT, POULTRY AND FISH

Deep-frying is a cooking method that makes many cooks apprehensive—both for safety reasons and because the results can be problematic. In fact, however, once you've mastered a few rules, deep-frying is both safe and simple and gives extremely appetizing results—tender, delicious foods with a crisp coating that produces a contrast in textures.

Equipment

To deep-fry, it is necessary to have a deep-fryer. Many consider an electric deep-fryer preferable, for the thermostatically controlled temperature gives perfect results. If you do not have an electric fryer, you will need a frying thermometer to gauge the temperature of the oil during the frying process. A frying basket in which the foods to be fried are placed so they can easily and quickly be lowered into the oil or lifted out is very useful but not absolutely essential. If you don't have one, use a slotted metal spoon to lift foods out of the oil.

You may also want to try deep-frying in a wok. Its width makes it a most efficient tool for this form of cooking. Use a skimmer to remove the fried pieces.

Foods for Deep Frying

Because this is a fast cooking method, only tender meats, poultry and fish may be used successfully. Chicken or turkey portions, whole or boned, flattened and stuffed, can be used for a variety of dishes, as can veal and pork scallops. Fish are particularly delicious deep-fried, and some shellfish are good this way, too. Croquettes and fritters, made from an enormous variety of ingredients, freshly cooked or leftovers, are usually deep-fried and can be served as first course or main dish.

Fats and Oils for Deep-Frying

The first consideration is the burning point of the fat. A fat with a low burning point, such as butter, cannot be used. Even clarified butter, which has a higher burning point than unclarified butter, cannot be heated to a high enough temperature for deep-frying.

Olive oil has a high burning point and is much favored in Mediterranean countries, but its strong smell and taste might be overwhelming for Americans. Some animal fats—lard from pork and sometimes suet from beef—are used for deep-frying, but the taste is not suitable for all foods, and the problem of cholesterol makes these less desirable. The best choices are vegetable oils, such as peanut and corn, or the various polyunsaturated oils marketed for cooking. These oils have a very high burning point and do not impart tastes to the foods; in fact, they enhance the natural flavor while giving a crisp finish. Vegetable shortenings may also be used.

When filling the deep-fryer, never fill it to the top, but only about halfway, so there is no possibility of the oil bubbling over and causing fires or burns. If you are using a thermostatically controlled electric fryer, you may fill it more than half full, as the steady controlled temperature usually prevents bubbling over, but it should still not be full. In any fryer there can be spatters when you drop in the coated food or lower the basket.

Before you begin to fry, measure the capacity of your fryer so you know how much oil or fat will be required.

Coatings

In order to protect the outer surface of the food from the drying effect of the hot oil, foods to be deep-fried should be coated.

The food can be dipped into flour or crumbs, without other preparation, or it can be dipped into milk, then into flour or crumbs. For a heavier coating, foods can be dipped into beaten whole egg or an egg-white coating and then into crumbs. An *anglaise* coating is a mixture of whole egg, oil and water beaten together. The Japanese tempura batter uses whole egg also, but no oil. Finally, there are thick batters, mixtures made with some starch (flour or cornstarch), which make thicker coatings.

Egg and Crumb Coating. This can be used for chicken, turkey, veal and pork scallops, fish, shellfish and croquettes. Often the food is first dusted with a very thin coating of flour; the flour can be applied with a dredger, or the pieces can be dipped or rolled in flour. Larger pieces, such as chicken portions, can be placed one by one in a flour-filled plastic bag; coat by shaking the bag.

The flour for this coating can be plain, or it can be seasoned or flavored with crumbled dried herbs. For seasoning, add ½ to 1 teaspoon salt and a few grinds of black pepper and/or cayenne pepper to 1 cup flour. For flavoring, use the grated rind of 1 lemon, 1 teaspoon dried rosemary, 1 tablespoon minced fresh parsley, or other herbs of your choice.

Egg can be used alone or beaten with a little water. Do not overbeat the egg; just stir quickly with a fork to break down the membranes of both yolk and white and combine them well. For 4 portions of food, allow 1 large egg; if the recipe directs you to add water, it will usually be 1 tablespoon water per egg.

The bread crumbs must be fine, whether fresh or dried. You will need about 1½ cups to coat 4 portions, or 1 pound of food. It is wise to dip food twice into egg and crumbs to be sure it is well insulated from the frying fat; dip pieces into egg, into crumbs, then into egg and into crumbs again.

After a food has been coated with crumbs, it should be chilled to set the coating so it adheres to the food and the crumbs don't fall away and burn in the hot fat. Cover the food loosely—tight wrapping will prevent the crumbs from sticking properly—and refrigerate. Do not put coated foods straight from the refrigerator into the kettle of oil; this can cause spattering from the moisture in the cold food and, more important, it will reduce the temperature of the oil and the food will become fat-logged. After the food has been chilled for 1 hour, leave it on a wire rack at room temperature for 15 minutes to ½ hour before starting to fry.

Batter Coating. Batter coating can be used for fritters, croquettes, cubes or slices of meat, poultry and fish, or whole sausages. It is not recommended for thicker pieces of food as the batter may be overcooked before the food is cooked in the center. You will need about 2 cups batter for 4 portions, or 1 pound of food.

Plain Fritter Batter produces a fairly heavy coating. If a lighter coating is preferred, egg whites can be added or beer or carbonated water used for the liquid. When the beer batter is mixed, it is set aside to ferment, which will make the batter even lighter. Beaten egg white is usually added to beer batters; fold it in just before you are ready to use the batter.

Japanese Tempura Batter contains a whole egg and gives a deep golden color to foods. Although it is a heavy batter, it produces light, delicate and crisp results.

Batter can stick to the frying basket and burn, so batter-coated foods are most often just dropped directly into the hot oil, a few pieces at a time. However, it is possible to use the basket and avoid sticking by dipping it into the hot oil for a few seconds before placing batter-coated foods in it.

How to Make Batters

Fritter batter is made with all-purpose flour. The leavening is generally provided by air and egg whites.

Plain Fritter Batter. For 2 cups plain batter, you will need 1 cup of flour. Sift to remove lumps and to incorporate air, which will help make the batter crisp. Sift a pinch of salt with the flour. Make a well in the center of the flour and pour in 2 tablespoons olive or vegetable oil and ⅔ cup cold water. Using a wooden spoon, gradually bring the flour into the well and continue mixing until the batter has the texture of thickened cream.

To lighten this plain batter, add 2 beaten egg whites per 2 cups batter. Beat the whites until stiff but not dry and fold the batter and egg whites together. Use promptly before the air escapes and the batter deflates.

Beer Batter. Beer or carbonated (sparkling) water can be used in place of cold water to give an even lighter batter. When beer is used, the batter is left to stand before use so that it can ferment slightly, which will aerate the mixture and thus lighten it. When ready to use the batter, add beaten egg whites as described above. Because there is no fermentation with carbonated water, add the egg whites as

Fritter Batter

makes about 2 cups

1	cup all-purpose flour
	pinch of salt
2	tablespoons olive oil
⅔	cup cold water
2	large egg whites (optional)

1 Sift flour and salt into a bowl.

2 Make a well in the center. Pour olive oil and water into the well. Gradually mix in flour from the sides.

soon as the batter is mixed and use promptly.

Japanese Tempura Batter. This batter has whole egg in it. Instead of adding egg to flour, add flour to egg. Unlike some other batters, which are improved by resting, this batter should be used as soon as it is ready. Measure the water and chill it in the refrigerator for 2 hours, or put ice cubes in a jug of water and measure the water out of the jug when the ice has melted. Measure 1 cup all-purpose flour and sift it with a pinch of salt into a bowl. Break 1 large egg into a larger bowl, add 1 tablespoon soy sauce, and whisk to blend. Pour in ⅔ cup ice water, a little at a time, whisking after each addition. Finally add the sifted flour, 1 tablespoon at a time, whisking as you add. Continue until all the flour is incorporated and the batter is smooth and creamy. Use immediately.

How to Deep-Fry

The dangers of deep-fat frying can be dealt with easily if you use caution and follow a few simple rules. Never leave a deep-fryer unattended. Always have on hand a metal lid to cover the deep-fryer should the oil become too hot and ignite, and a box of baking soda to sprinkle on any flames should flaming oil spatter outside the pan. Never attempt to put out an oil fire with water; water will make the oil spatter and the fire will spread.

Pour the oil into the fryer, but remember to leave space for the oil to froth up, as it will when food is added. Place at least 3 inches of oil in the fryer. Heat the oil gradually over moderate heat, and do not let it become overheated. Overheated oil can give an unpleasant taste to the food and can overcook the outside before the inside is done. Overheated oil can also burst into flames. Heat the oil exactly to the required temperature. For raw foods, the temperature should be 360°F. When the food is added, the temperature of the oil will be reduced for a few seconds, but it will soon return to the proper level. For cooked foods, such as croquettes or fritters made with already cooked meat, poultry or fish, heat the oil to 375°F. These foods need only enough time in the oil to cook the coating and heat the interior, and therefore they must be fried at a higher temperature to insure that they brown well in this short time. Small raw shellfish, such as shrimps, clams or oysters, also need the higher temperature, 375°F, since the cooking time for these is also brief.

Make sure your thermometer, spoons and basket are dry before putting them into the oil, as water makes the fat spit, which can cause burns.

Do not fry too much at one time. Adding too many pieces of food at once lowers the temperature of the oil, slows the cooking, prevents proper sealing of the food, and will result in an oily taste. Unless your fryer is thermostatically controlled, check the temperature frequently. If it is too cool, increase heat slightly. If it is too hot, pour in a few tablespoons of fresh oil.

Turn the food as it cooks. When it has puffed and browned and has cooked the length of time specified in the recipe, quickly lift out and test a piece. If it is ready, remove the rest of the fried pieces and drain on paper towels. If you are frying several batches, keep the already fried batches warm on a baking sheet lined with paper towels in a 250° to 300°F oven. Take care to return the oil to the correct frying temperature before starting to cook the next batch. Do not keep the food in the oven too long because the crisp outside starts to become soft and the inside can become soggy.

Preparing and Frying Stuffed Meats

For stuffing, use chicken and turkey leg and breast portions, and veal and pork scallops. Bone chicken breasts and legs for easier serving. A small piece of bone can be left at the bottom of the leg to serve as a handle, but the bone should be covered with foil to keep it from being breaded or covered with batter, and to keep it from becoming too oily in frying. The boneless breast portions can be flattened like a scallop,

3 Mix the batter to the consistency of thickened cream. Let it rest for 30 minutes.

4 If using egg whites, beat them until stiff but not dry. Fold the batter and whites together. Use immediately.

Tempura Batter

makes 1¼ cups

1	cup all-purpose flour
	pinch of salt
1	large egg
1	tablespoon soy sauce
⅔	cup ice water

1 Sift the flour and salt into a bowl.

2 Break the egg into a bowl. Add the soy sauce and whisk to blend. Still whisking, add ice water, a little at a time.

3 Add flour to liquids, 1 tablespoon at a time. Whisk vigorously after each addition. Use batter immediately.

ters well in advance of use and chill for at least 2 hours.

Other excellent stuffings are cheese—Gruyère, Fontina, Edam, or any cheese that melts easily—or a highly flavored meat whose color contrasts with the meat being stuffed: prosciutto with veal and ham or tongue with chicken and turkey, for example.

Roll or fold the meat around the stuffing, making sure it is completely enclosed. Butter or cheese, if not completely enclosed, will melt into the hot oil during frying. Although the natural protein of the meat or poultry usually holds the little rolls together, it is always a good precaution to fasten them with wooden toothpicks (do not use plastic for frying) or stainless-steel poultry pins. These should be removed before serving. If you have left a little bone handle in a chicken leg and wrapped it in foil, the foil can be replaced with a paper frill for serving.

Flattened pieces of meat have been beaten out to such a thin layer that they cook quickly even when stuffed. Allow 5 to 8 minutes for a stuffed flattened chicken breast or a veal scallop. If you overcook it, the meat will develop a leathery texture and start to shrink and release the stuffing. When you think the meat is done quickly remove a piece and make a small cut in the surface of the meat to be sure it is cooked as you like it, but do not pierce deeply into the butter- or cheese-stuffed packages with a skewer or a knife, or the stuffing will melt and run out.

but poultry does not flatten as easily as veal or pork and the poultry scallop will never be as thin or as flexible. Turkey breasts are so large and thick that it is best to slice them and flatten the slices.

For stuffing with flavored butter, allow about 1 ounce for each individual portion, although more or less can be used according to taste and the size of the piece of meat or poultry. Good

stuffing choices are Garlic Butter, Maître d'Hôtel Butter and Mustard Butter (see Volume 1 Index for Compound Butters). Sage Butter is made by adding 1 teaspoon minced fresh sage and a few drops of lemon juice to 2 tablespoons butter. Orange Butter, particularly good with pork, is made by adding the grated rind and juice of 1 orange to 8 tablespoons butter. Prepare all but-

Preparing and Frying Fish

Fish is delicious when deep-fried. If it is done well, the result is crispy, grease-free, and tender. For best results, the fish should not be more than 1 inch thick, but it may be a whole small fish, a fillet or a chunk. Fish can also be flaked to make fritters or croquettes, and can be mixed with potatoes to make fish cakes or balls.

Small whole fish such as sardines, smelts, dabs, flounders, perch

Boning and Stuffing Chicken Portions

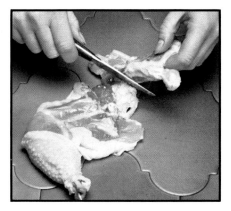

1 If there are any small rib bones attached to the breast portions of the chicken, remove them.

2 Roll flesh away to expose leg bone. Cut down the leg to middle of drumstick.

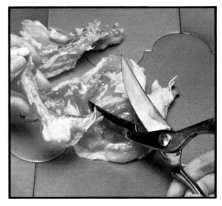

3 With poultry shears cut through the leg bone halfway down the drumstick.

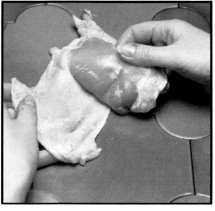

4 Pull the leg bones away, leaving the small broken bone in place. Remove skin.

5 Beat the meat flat between 2 pieces of wax paper. (Avoid the bone while flattening the meat.)

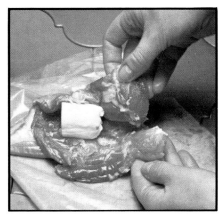

6 Place 1 ounce of stuffing in the center of each boned chicken portion. Wrap the meat around the stuffing.

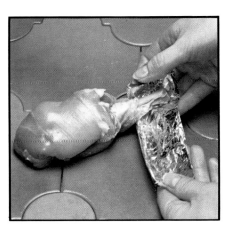

7 Tuck in any ends so the stuffing is enclosed by the meat. Cover the end bone with foil.

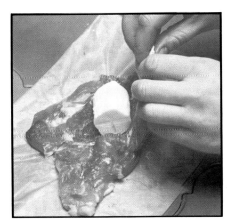

8 If using boneless portions, wrap the meat around the stuffing to make a football shape.

9 Roll chicken in seasoned flour. Coat twice with egg and crumbs. Chill, then leave at room temperature for 1 hour before frying.

and butterfish and shellfish such as clams, oysters and shrimps are good choices. Fillets of cod, haddock, hake and flounder and chunks of larger fish such as halibut, monkfish, shark and swordfish are all good for deep-frying.

All fish for frying must be enclosed in a substantial egg and bread crumb or batter coating. The plain Fritter Batter can be used alone, or can be lightened with egg white. Beer Batter is very good with fish and shellfish, as is Tempura Batter, which is also useful for any of the vegetables often served with tempura foods.

Scale and gut the whole fish; remove heads, tails and fins. If you like, about 1 hour in advance sprinkle the inside of the fish with salt and pepper, and add any flavorings. Shell and devein shrimps, leaving the last tail section in place if you prefer; this little tail piece can serve as a sort of handle. Scrub and shuck clams, mussels and oysters. Skin fillets if not already skinless; they can be cut into smaller portions or even sliced if they are thicker than 1 inch. Cut chunks from steaks or fillets. Be sure that any steak or fillet is boneless.

When ready to fry, dust the fish lightly with flour and shake gently or toss in a sieve to remove any excess flour. Do not flour fish in advance, lest the flour absorb moisture from the fish and become soggy. Coat the fish with

Scotch Eggs

4 portions

4	large eggs, hard-cooked
2	teaspoons flour seasoned with salt and freshly ground pepper
1	pound pork sausage meat dash of Worcestershire sauce
1	large raw egg
2	cups fresh white bread crumbs
	oil for deep-frying

1 Shell the hard-cooked eggs. Place seasoned flour on a plate.

2 Roll eggs in the flour to coat them evenly. Shake off excess flour.

6 Continue until egg is covered with an even coating of sausage meat. Repeat with other eggs.

7 Roll coated eggs in remaining flour. Break the raw egg into a bowl and beat lightly.

8 Dip Scotch eggs into beaten egg. Place bread crumbs in a large plastic bag.

egg and crumbs. If you are using a batter coating, dip the fish into the batter just before frying.

Heat the oil to the correct temperature. Place crumb-coated fish or shellfish, a few at a time, in the frying basket. Batter-coated pieces can be dropped directly into the oil, or the basket can be first dipped into the oil for a few seconds and then filled with a few of the pieces. Use tongs both to pick up the pieces for dipping into the batter

and also to drop them into the oil. As an alternative, lift them on a sturdy fork without piercing them, resting the piece on the fork tines.

Fry the fish for 3 to 5 minutes, depending on the thickness of the piece, or until the coating is crisp and golden brown and the fish cooked through. Check by quickly removing one piece and testing it with a fork to see if the fish flakes. If you are frying very small pieces, 1 or 2 minutes may

be enough. Turn the fish or shellfish once, using a slotted spoon or chopsticks. Lift the finished pieces out with a slotted spoon and drain on paper towels.

Serve deep-fried fish and shellfish on a serving plate or in a basket lined with a paper doily to absorb the last drops of oil. Lemon wedges or slices are usually served with fried fish, but you may choose other garnishes; cherry tomatoes, cucumber strips or slices,

3 Place sausage meat in a large bowl. Add Worcestershire sauce and mix well.

4 Divide meat into 4 portions. With floured hands form each portion into a flat patty.

5 Place a floured egg in the center of a sausage patty and bring the meat up around the egg.

9 Toss Scotch eggs, one at a time, in the bag of crumbs. Repeat egg and crumb procedure

10 Heat the oil to 360°F or until a 1-inch cube of bread browns in 55 seconds.

11 Fry the Scotch eggs, two at a time, for about 10 minutes, or until well browned.

watercress and parsley sprigs are all good.

Scotch Eggs

This British specialty is a stuffed item, almost like a croquette. Hard-cooked eggs are surrounded by sausage meat, dipped into raw egg and crumbs, and fried until crisp. For this, use good-quality bulk sausage meat. If that proves difficult to buy, use good sausages and remove the meat from the casings. You will need about 4 ounces of sausage meat for each egg. The sausage can be flavored with minced fresh sage, snipped chives, or other flavorings of your choice.

Fritters

Fritters are made from small portions of meat, poultry, fish or vegetables enclosed in a batter (we will only deal with vegetables here when they are part of a meat or fish fry), or the same ingredient chopped or ground and mixed into the batter. They are not shaped, but are dropped by spoonfuls into the hot oil, and their lumpy contours make them the more attractive.

Fritter batter is similar to pancake batter, but pancakes should be elastic in texture whereas fritter batter is intended to provide a crisp coating. This batter must therefore be very light, incorporating extra air with beaten egg whites, yeast, or a carbonated beverage. Any light batter can be used for fritters.

When the batter is ready, the main ingredient is stirred in and mixed well. This can be chopped or ground chicken, turkey, or ham. Since fritters are most often made from already cooked ingredients, or from quickly cooked ingredients, the oil should be heated to 375°F and the cooking should be brief—3 to 5 minutes is usually enough, but the exact time depends on the size of the fritter. Very small spoonfuls of batter will cook in the shortest time, perhaps only 2 minutes.

For the kind of fritter that is actually a batter-coated shellfish, the main ingredients must be quite dry; in the case of Fritto Misto the ingredients are dipped into flour just before being coated with batter. In the case of Tempura, the ingredients are simply dried. When the batter and oil are ready, individual pieces are picked up with tongs, dipped into batter, and then dropped into the hot oil. The frying time depends on the individual food, but it is always brief, 3 to 5 minutes for whole shrimps, 2 to 4 minutes for oysters, 2 to 3 minutes for clams, 2 minutes for smaller items such as mushrooms.

Drain finished fritters on paper towels and keep them warm in a low oven until all are ready.

Croquettes

Croquettes are always made from already cooked ingredients; these may be leftovers or freshly cooked. The main ingredient is bound with mashed potatoes, a panada (bread crumb mixture), or a thick flour-based sauce. Croquettes are usually shaped like corks, often with one end fatter than the other, but they can be molded into any shape you like.

The croquette mixture should be chilled to be firm enough to shape; allow 30 minutes to 1 hour for this. Then shape the croquettes, using about 3 heaping tablespoons of the mixture for each one. Roll and shape them on a floured board or with floured hands, which will give them a very thin flour coating. Coat them with a double thickness of egg and crumbs and arrange them in a single layer, not touching each other, on a flat surface. The shaped croquettes should be chilled to become firm; even if you are short of time, allow at least an hour, but several hours or overnight is better. Before frying, leave them at room temperature for at least an hour.

Fry croquettes in oil heated to 375°F. They need only a few minutes—5 to 6 minutes for croquettes made as described, but less time if you have made them smaller. Remember that because all the ingredients are already cooked, the frying serves only to heat them and make the coating puffy and golden.

Mashed Potato Croquettes. Use equal quantities of mashed potato and all the other ingredients combined (chopped or ground meat, flavorings and egg yolk or whole egg). The meat should be chopped or ground very fine. Good flavorings are grated cheese, minced scallions, herbs, crumbled bacon, chopped peanuts. Flavoring vegetables can be added, but use cautiously as the moisture in tomatoes and green peppers can make the croquette mixture too soft. The mashed potato must be firm, not soupy. To make it absolutely smooth, put it through a food mill or ricer or purée in a food processor. Combine all the ingredients, chill until firm, and mold.

Panada Croquettes. To make a panada (which comes from *pan*, the Spanish word for bread), remove crusts from 3 or 4 slices of fresh bread and reduce the bread to crumbs; there should be about 2 cups of crumbs. Turn crumbs into a saucepan and pour in ½ cup milk. Heat the mixture to lukewarm, making sure all the crumbs are moistened, then remove from heat and cool until you can handle the mixture. Lift out the moistened bread and squeeze out the milk. Put the bread paste in a shallow bowl and mash with a fork. Combine with an equal volume of ground meat or poultry and the flavoring ingredients. Mix well, cool, shape into balls or cork shapes, and coat with flour. These croquettes are not usually coated with egg and crumbs, but they can be if you wish.

Croquettes Bound with a Flour-Based Sauce. In France, this thick sauce is also called a *panade*. For 4 portions make a white sauce with 3 tablespoons butter, 3 tablespoons flour and ¾ cup milk. Thicken it further with 2 large egg yolks. Stir in 12 ounces to 1¼ pounds of meat or poultry, trimmed and chopped or ground. Add grated cheese or flavoring ingredients. Chill the mixture, shape it, coat with egg and crumbs, and chill again. Leave out at room temperature for an hour before frying.

For some recipes milk should be replaced by brown stock, veal stock or game stock, according to the main ingredient.

Turkey Fritters

makes 14 fritters

¾	cup all-purpose flour	12	ounces boneless cooked turkey
¾	teaspoon salt	1	lemon
¾	teaspoon freshly ground pepper	2	large egg whites
1	tablespoon butter		oil for deep-frying
1½	teaspoons curry powder		mango chutney
⅔	cup warm water		

Sift the flour and salt into a bowl. Add the pepper. Melt the butter in a small saucepan. Add the curry powder and sauté for 2 minutes over low heat. Make a well in the center of the flour and pour in the butter. Gradually add the warm water and work the flour in from the sides. Mix to make a smooth, thick batter. Remove any skin or tendon from the turkey and mince the meat. Stir it into the batter. Grate the lemon rind to measure 2 teaspoons and add to the batter. Whisk the egg whites until they stand in stiff peaks, then fold them into the batter. Preheat the oven to 250°F and line a baking sheet with paper towels.

Heat the oil in a deep-fryer to 360°F. In several batches, scoop up tablespoons of the batter and lower them into the oil, or arrange them in a frying basket, and fry for about 4 minutes, or until golden brown. Turn at least once during cooking. Lift fritters out, lay on baking sheet to drain and keep warm in oven until all the fritters have been fried. Serve immediately, accompanied by mango chutney.

Beer Batter

makes about 2 cups

1 cup all-purpose flour
 pinch of salt
2 tablespoons olive oil

⅔ cup beer or light ale
1 large egg white

Sift flour and salt into a bowl. Make a well in the center and pour the oil and beer into the well. Gradually stir in the flour from the sides until the mixture is thick and smooth. Let the batter rest for 2 hours.

Beat the egg white until stiff but not dry. Fold the egg white into the batter. Use immediately.
Variation: Substitute sparkling water for the beer, omit the refrigeration period, add the beaten egg white and use immediately.

Egg-White Coating

Especially good for fish.

makes about 1¼ cups

3 large egg whites
6 tablespoons olive or peanut
 oil

1 tablespoon fresh lemon
 juice
1 tablespoon light soy sauce*

Drop the egg whites into a blender container and pour in the oil, lemon juice and soy sauce. Add 2 tablespoons warm, not hot, water. Blend the mixture until smooth. If it is too thick, add more warm water, 1 tablespoon at a time, and blend. The mixture should be thick but not stiff.

Dip foods into the coating, and then coat them with fine crumbs.
*This kind of soy sauce is lighter-bodied and less dense-tasting. Ask for it in Oriental markets, or buy a Japanese brand of soy sauce at the supermarket.

Anglaise Coating

This coating is good for panfrying as well as deep-frying.

makes about ¼ cup

1 whole egg
2 teaspoons oil

1 teaspoon water
 salt and freshly ground pepper

Drop the egg, oil and water into a blender container and whirl until the ingredients are completely mixed. Season lightly with salt and pepper.

Flour the foods very lightly, then brush them with the anglaise coating, making a thin layer. Coat with crumbs.

Veal and Cheese Rolls with Garlic-Parsley Butter

4 portions

8 veal scallops, each about 2
 ounces
12 tablespoons unsalted
 butter, at room
 temperature
2 large garlic cloves
1 lemon
4 tablespoons minced fresh
 parsley

8 thin slices of Gruyère or
 Fontina cheese
½ cup all-purpose flour
½ teaspoon salt
¼ teaspoon freshly ground
 pepper
1 large egg
3 slices of fresh white bread
 oil for deep-frying

Pound the veal scallops between sheets of wax paper so they are almost doubled in size. Place the softened butter in a bowl and beat until creamy. Peel the garlic and put through a press into the butter. Squeeze the lemon to measure 1 teaspoon juice and add to butter along with parsley. Mix well. Spread the butter over the slices of veal and place a slice of cheese over the butter coating. Roll up the scallops like a jelly roll and tuck in the ends. If necessary, fasten with wooden toothpicks or stainless-steel poultry pins.

Combine the flour with the salt and pepper. Put the seasoned flour on a plate. Beat the egg and pour into a shallow bowl. Put the bread in the blender or food processor and reduce to fine crumbs. Measure out 1¼ cups. Put the bread crumbs in a plastic bag. Coat the veal rolls with the seasoned flour, then dip into the beaten egg, and finally shake them, one at a time, in the bag of crumbs until they are evenly coated. Repeat the egg and crumb coating. Arrange the rolls in a single layer on a plate, cover lightly and chill for 2 hours. Remove from the refrigerator ½ hour before frying.

Preheat the oven to 250°F and line a baking sheet with paper towels. Heat the oil in a deep-fryer to 360°F. Fry half the veal rolls at a time for 5 to 8 minutes, until brown and crisp on the outside. Turn during cooking. Transfer cooked rolls to baking sheet and keep warm in oven as you fry the rest. Be careful not to overcook the veal, as the layer of meat is very thin.

Variations: Use a slice of ham or prosciutto instead of cheese.

Spread the veal with chive butter instead of parsley and garlic butter.

Fried Clams

6 portions

2	recipes of Fritter Batter*		oil for deep-frying
4	dozen softshell clams		lemon wedges

Make a double batch of the batter and let it rest for 40 minutes. Preheat oven to 250°F and line a baking sheet with paper towels. Open the clam shells and remove the clams; be careful to pick out all bits of shell. Place clams on several thicknesses of paper towels. Turn them on the paper towels to dry them well. Pour oil into a deep-fryer and heat to 375°F. Beat the 4 egg whites until stiff but not dry, and fold them into the batter.

When the oil has reached 375°F, start dipping the clams into the batter. Drop them, six to eight at a time, into the hot oil and fry for 2 minutes, or until they are golden brown. Transfer them to the baking sheet as they are done. Keep warm in oven. Serve them piping hot, garnished with lemon wedges. Accompany with tartar sauce.

*Mix the flour, salt, olive oil and water as directed in the Fritter Batter recipe, but reserve the 4 egg whites until called for.

Chinese Sweet-and-Sour Pork

4 portions

	Sweet-and-Sour Sauce		Batter
2	tablespoons oil	1	cup all-purpose flour
1	medium-size onion	1	teaspoon baking powder
1	green bell pepper	1	teaspoon salt
4	teaspoons cornstarch	1	egg
1¼	cups Chicken Stock (see Volume 1 Index) or canned broth	½	teaspoon peanut oil
		⅔	cup cold water
2	tablespoons tomato purée		
1	can (8 ounces) apricot halves		
6	tablespoons golden raisins	1	pound pork tenderloin
1	tablespoon honey		flour
3	tablespoons red-wine vinegar		oil for deep-frying
	pinch of salt		
½	teaspoon ground ginger		

Make the sauce: Pour the oil into a heavy saucepan. Peel the onion and grate into the oil. Sauté gently for about 3 minutes over low heat. Wash and halve the green pepper, discard stem, seeds and ribs, and chop the pepper. Add to the onion and sauté for 3 minutes longer. Blend the cornstarch with a little of the stock. Stir the rest of the stock into the cornstarch along with the tomato purée and, still stirring, add gradually to the saucepan. Continue to stir and cook for about 5 minutes, or until thickened. Drain the apricots, reserving the syrup, and set the apricots aside. Add the reserved syrup and remaining sauce ingredients to the saucepan. Cover the pan and simmer gently for about 20 minutes. Chop the apricots and add for the last 5 minutes. Set the sauce aside.

Make the batter: Sift the flour, baking powder and salt into a bowl. Beat the egg. Make a well in the center of the flour and drop in the egg and the peanut oil. Gradually work the flour into the egg and oil mixture. Slowly beat in the cold water. Let the batter stand for 20 minutes.

Cut the pork tenderloin into ½-inch crosswise slices. If the slices are large toward the thicker end, halve them. Dip the pieces in a little flour, then stir them into the batter.

Preheat the oven to 250°F and line a baking sheet with paper towels. Heat the oil in a deep-fryer to 360°F. Letting excess batter drip off, fry the coated pork pieces, a few at a time, for 10 minutes per batch, turning at least once. When browned, transfer to the baking sheet and keep warm in oven while frying the remaining pieces.

Reheat the sauce and serve it poured over the pork or alongside it, and accompany the meat with rice.

Maryland Crab Cakes

4 portions

6	slices of firm white bread
⅔	cup water
16	saltines
1	pound lump crab meat, fresh, frozen or pasteurized
3	large eggs
1	tablespoon Dijon-style mustard
3	tablespoons minced fresh parsley
	salt and freshly ground pepper
	cayenne pepper or Tabasco® (optional)
	oil for deep-frying
	lime wedges

Remove crusts from the bread and whirl the bread in a blender or food processor until reduced to crumbs; there should be about 3 cups of crumbs. Put crumbs in a saucepan and pour in the water, just enough to moisten all the crumbs. Bring to just under a boil, then remove from heat and cool. Squeeze the crumbs to remove the water and put the moistened crumbs (the panada) in a bowl. Mash the crumbs with a fork. In a blender or a food processor, reduce the saltines to very fine crumbs and set aside.

Pick over the crab meat, removing any bits of cartilage. Add crab to the bread crumbs. Beat 2 of the eggs and mix in the mustard. Pour the eggs into the bread crumb and crab mixture and add the parsley. Mix everything together until well combined. Taste, and season as you like. Most people like crab cakes a little spicy; if you do, add cayenne pepper or Tabasco to taste. Chill the mixture for 30 minutes.

Beat the remaining egg with 1 tablespoon water. Spread the saltine crumbs on a sheet of wax paper. Shape the crab mixture into 12 small balls, and flatten the balls. Dip them into the beaten egg, then roll in the crumbs until well covered. Chill the cakes for 1 hour.

A half hour before frying, remove crab cakes from refrigerator. Preheat oven to 250°F and line a baking sheet with paper towels. Heat the oil in a deep-fryer to 375°F. Place 6 cakes at a time in the frying basket and fry for about 4 minutes or until golden brown. Turn the cakes with chopsticks after 2 minutes. Lift out and place on a baking sheet. Keep warm in oven as you finish frying. Serve crab cakes with wedges of lime.

Kromeskies

(Russian Chicken Croquettes)

4 portions

Filling	Batter

Filling

1	large green bell pepper
8	ounces boneless cooked chicken
4	tablespoons butter
½	cup all-purpose flour
1¼	cups milk
1	large egg yolk
	salt and pepper

Batter

1	cup all-purpose flour
1	teaspoon salt
1	tablespoon corn oil
⅔	cup warm water
1	large egg white
8	slices of lean bacon
	oil for deep-frying

Make the filling: Use a swivel peeler to remove as much of the skin as possible from the green pepper. Cut pepper into quarters and discard stem, seeds and ribs. Chop the pepper. Remove any skin or tendon from the chicken and chop chicken into small pieces. Set chopped ingredients aside. Melt the butter in a heavy pan over low heat. Add the flour and cook, stirring, for 3 minutes, but do not let the roux brown. Warm the milk and, off the heat, pour it gradually into the roux. Return to heat and cook for 4 minutes, stirring. Beat in the egg yolk and season with salt and pepper to taste. Stir the chopped green pepper and chicken into the sauce, mix well, and check the seasoning. Remove from heat and leave until cold. Cover lightly and chill for at least 1 hour.

Divide the chicken mixture into 8 portions. Flour your hands and shape each portion into a croquette. Cover lightly and chill for at least 1 hour. Remove from refrigerator about ½ hour before frying.

Make the batter: Sift the flour and salt into a bowl. Make a well in the center and pour in the oil and warm water. Work in the flour from the sides, then beat until all ingredients are blended. Set aside in a cool place—not the refrigerator—for at least 1 hour.

Wrap each croquette in a bacon strip and secure with a wooden toothpick. Whisk the egg white until it stands in stiff peaks. Fold the egg white into the cold batter. Preheat the oven to 250°F and line a baking sheet with paper towels.

Heat the oil in a deep-fryer until it reaches 375°F. Using tongs, dip each croquette into the batter and let excess drip off. Deep-fry the croquettes for about 5 minutes or until puffy and golden. Turn at least once during cooking. Lift from the oil and drain on paper towels. When all the kromeskies are fried, serve them piping hot.

Japanese Tempura

The foods chosen for frying in tempura batter should have contrasting colors, flavors and textures; Japanese cooks vary the ingredients according to season and availability, using such things as cod, eel, flounder, snapper, crabs, scallops, shrimps, squids, bamboo shoots, cauliflower, eggplant, green pepper, lotus root, mushrooms. Serve tempura with other Japanese dishes, or with rice.

4 portions

12	large fresh shrimps
12	fresh mussels
4	scallions
12	green beans
12	snow peas

Stuffed Mushrooms

1	dried black mushroom
6	fresh shrimps
3	fresh or canned water chestnuts
2	scallions
½	cup bean sprouts
8	large mushrooms
1	ounce fresh gingerroot
	salt

2 cups Tempura Batter
oil for deep-frying

lemon wedges and parsley
sprigs for garnish

Tempura Sauce

2 ounces fresh gingerroot
1 cup light soy sauce*
6 tablespoons granulated
sugar
½ lemon or lime
1 cup dry sherry wine
1 cup vegetable stock

Shell and devein the 12 shrimps; if you like, leave the last tail section in place. Score the underside of the shrimps to prevent their curling during frying. Scrub mussels in several changes of water, remove beards, and put in a heavy pan with ¼ cup water. Set the pan over high heat and shake it for about 5 minutes, or until the mussels have opened. Remove from shells, discarding any mussels that have not opened. Trim ends of scallions, beans and snow peas; wash vegetables and roll in paper towels to dry. Arrange the shellfish and vegetables on a plate and cover and chill. Remove from the refrigerator 30 minutes before frying.

Prepare the stuffed mushrooms: Put the dried mushroom in a bowl and pour boiling water over it to cover. Soak for 20 minutes. Shell and devein the 6 shrimps and chop into very small pieces. If using fresh water chestnuts, peel them. Cut water chestnuts into thin slices and the slices into thin strips. Trim and mince the scallions. Rinse the bean sprouts and chop them into rough pieces. Drain the soaked dried mushroom, discard the tough stem, and mince the cap. Wipe the fresh mushrooms with a damp cloth or paper towel and trim base of stems. Twist out the stems and chop them. Peel and grate the gingerroot. Combine all the stuffing in-

gredients in a mixing bowl and season with salt. Fill the fresh mushroom caps with the mixture and press to make the filling firm. Arrange mushrooms on the plate with the rest of the tempura ingredients, cover lightly and chill.

Preheat the oven to 250°F and line a baking sheet with paper towels. Heat the oil in a deep-fryer to 360°F. Dip individual pieces of shellfish, vegetable and stuffed mushrooms into the batter and at once transfer to the hot oil. Deep-fry in small batches, turning the pieces once or twice until golden brown. Drain on a rack, then transfer to the baking sheet and keep hot in the oven until all the pieces are fried.

Make the tempura sauce: Squeeze the lemon or lime. Peel the gingerroot and grate. Put slices and lemon juice in a large screw-top jar, at least 4-cup size, and add all the other sauce ingredients. Shake to mix. Pour into 4 individual bowls.

Serve the fried foods on a large warmed serving plate, garnished with lemon wedges and parsley sprigs. Give each person a bowl of sauce.

*Buy light soy sauce in Oriental markets, or buy a Japanese brand of soy sauce at the supermarket.

Monkfish Scampi

(Mock Lobsterettes)

The monkfish, or goosefish, is a rather ugly fish of which only the tail meat is used. This can be cut into small pieces and fried to make imitation lobsterettes, or scampi in Italian.

6 portions

2	pounds monkfish tail
½	cup all-purpose flour
½	teaspoon salt
½	teaspoon freshly ground pepper
2	large eggs
2	tablespoons water

3	to 4 slices of white bread
	oil for deep-frying
	parsley sprigs
	lemon wedges
1	recipe Tomato-Flavored Mayonnaise (see Volume 3 Index)

Cut the monkfish into 1½-inch pieces, about ½ inch thick. There should be about 60 pieces. Combine the flour, salt and pepper and put the seasoned flour on a sheet of wax paper. Break the eggs into a shallow bowl and add the water. Beat lightly with a fork to mix well. Whirl the bread in a blender to reduce it to fine crumbs. You should have about 2 cups. Pile the bread crumbs on a large sheet of wax paper. Dip the fish pieces into the flour, lifting the edge of the wax paper to help coat them all over. Using tongs, lift each piece of fish in turn, shake lightly to remove excess flour, and dip the piece into the beaten eggs. Then coat each piece with bread crumbs. Place the coated fish on a tray, in a single layer, cover loosely with wax paper, and chill for 1 hour.

At least 15 minutes before frying, remove the monkfish from the refrigerator. Preheat the oven to 250°F and line a baking sheet with paper towels. Heat the oil to 375°F. Carefully place a layer of fish pieces in the frying basket. Lower the basket gently into the oil and fry the mock *scampi* for 2 minutes, turning once, or until the coating becomes golden brown and crisp. Immediately lift out the basket, drain over the deep-fryer for 2 seconds, then tip the fish onto the baking sheet to drain. Put the baking sheet into the oven to keep hot. Check that the oil has returned to the correct frying temperature, then fry remaining batches of fish pieces and transfer to the oven in the same fashion.

When all the fish has been fried and drained, pile it on a hot serving platter lined with a paper doily. Garnish with parsley sprigs and lemon wedges and serve with the tomato mayonnaise.

Deep-Fried Flounder Strips

4 portions

8	boneless flounder fillets, each about 4 ounces	½	cup all-purpose flour
½	cup milk		oil for deep-frying
½	teaspoon salt	3	tablespoons butter
½	teaspoon freshly ground black pepper	3	tablespoons chopped fresh parsley
¼	teaspoon cayenne pepper		lemon slices

Cut the flounder fillets into strips about 3 inches long and 1 inch wide. These little strips are called *goujons* because they resemble whole little fish (gudgeons), which are fried in the same way. Pour the milk into a bowl and beat in the salt, black pepper and cayenne. Put the flour in a shallow bowl. Dip the fish strips into the seasoned milk, then into the flour. Shake off any excess flour and set the fish in a single layer on a large plate.

Preheat the oven to 250°F and line a baking sheet with paper towels. Heat the oil in a deep-fryer to 360°F. Place the coated fish strips, four or five at a time, in the frying basket and lower them into the oil. Fry them for 3 to 4 minutes, until golden brown and crisp, turning at least once. Transfer fish to the baking sheet to drain. Keep warm in the oven while you cook and drain remaining strips.

Melt the butter in a small pan over moderate heat. Add the parsley and sauté for 1 minute. Arrange the cooked pieces of fish on a warmed serving platter and sprinkle them with the buttered parsley. Garnish with lemon slices. Serve at once.

Ham Croquettes

Delicious served with tart cranberry sauce and an assortment of mustards.

4 portions

1½	cups Brown Stock (see Volume 1 Index)	1	teaspoon Dijon-style mustard
2	tablespoons butter	½	teaspoon salt
3	tablespoons flour	¼	teaspoon freshly ground pepper
12	ounces boneless cooked ham	1	egg yolk
2	tablespoons minced fresh parsley	4	to 5 slices of stale bread
			oil for deep-frying
		1	whole egg

Heat the brown stock. Melt the butter in a saucepan over moderate heat. Stir in the flour with a wooden spoon and cook, stirring, for 2 minutes. Remove pan from heat and gradually pour in the brown stock, stirring constantly. When the mixture is smooth, return pan to moderate heat and cook for 5 or 6 minutes, still stirring. Cool the sauce to lukewarm.

Trim any fat or gristle from the ham, cut it into chunks, then grind it in a food grinder or food processor. Stir the ground ham, parsley, mustard, salt, pepper and egg yolk into the sauce; mix well. Pour the mixture into a shallow bowl and refrigerate for 1 hour, or until completely cold. Place bread in a blender or food processor and reduce to fine crumbs. You should have about 1⅓ cups.

Remove ham from refrigerator. With floured hands, divide the mixture into 8 to 12 equal portions and roll and shape them into croquettes. Break the whole egg into a shallow bowl and beat lightly. Put the bread crumbs on a plate. Dip croquettes into the egg, then roll them in the bread crumbs. Cover lightly and refrigerate for 1 hour or more. Remove from the refrigerator 30 minutes before cooking.

Preheat oven to 250° and line a baking sheet with paper towels. Heat the oil in a deep-fryer to 375°F. Place the croquettes, a few at a time, in the frying basket and lower into the oil. Fry for 5 to 6 minutes, or until croquettes are crisp and brown all over. Turn at least once during cooking. Lay them on the baking sheet and place in the oven until all the croquettes have been fried.

42

Chicken Kiev

4 portions

12	tablespoons unsalted butter, at room temperature
1	tablespoon minced fresh parsley
1	tablespoon snipped fresh chives
½	teaspoon salt
½	teaspoon freshly ground pepper
1	garlic clove
4	whole chicken breasts, each about 1 pound, split, skinned, and boned
4	to 5 slices of stale bread
2	eggs
½	cup all-purpose flour
	oil for deep-frying

Place the butter in a bowl and cream it with a wooden spoon. Beat in the parsley, chives, salt and pepper. Peel the garlic and put through a press into the butter. Mix until herbs and seasonings are evenly distributed. Divide the butter mixture into eighths, one eighth for each breast half, and shape them into small ovals. (You may have to chill the butter briefly before you can shape it.) Refrigerate the butter ovals.

Place a chicken breast half between sheets of wax paper on a chopping board and pound it thin. Continue until all pieces are flattened. Wrap each chicken piece around a butter oval, turning in the sides, turning up the bottom and bringing down the top flap to enclose the butter completely.

Place the bread in a food processor or blender and reduce to fine crumbs. You should have about 2 cups. Beat the eggs in a shallow bowl. Put the flour and bread crumbs in other shallow bowls and set the bowls side by side on the countertop. Dip chicken breasts, one by one, first into the flour, then into the beaten eggs, finally into the bread crumbs. Make sure each piece is completely coated. Cover lightly and refrigerate chicken for at least 1 hour. Remove from refrigerator ½ hour before frying.

Preheat oven to 250°F, and line a baking sheet with paper towels. Heat the oil in a deep-fryer to 360°F. Place the chicken, two pieces at a time, in the frying basket and lower into the oil. Fry for 6 to 8 minutes or until chicken is golden brown all over. Turn at least once during cooking. As each batch is done, transfer the pieces to the baking sheet and place in oven until all have been fried. Serve immediately.

Batter-Fried Shrimps

6 portions

1½	pounds fresh shrimps in shells
2	eggs
6	tablespoons cornstarch
1	teaspoon salt
¼	teaspoon cayenne pepper
3	tablespoons water
	oil for deep-frying
	lemon wedges

Sherry-Soy Sauce

1	tablespoon wine vinegar
1	tablespoon soft brown sugar
1	tablespoon tomato purée
1	tablespoon soy sauce
1	tablespoon peanut oil
¼	teaspoon salt
4	tablespoons dry sherry wine
1	tablespoon cornstarch
½	cup cold water

Shell the shrimps except for the final tail section, and devein them. Drain on paper towels. Separate the eggs. In a mixing bowl combine the cornstarch, salt and cayenne. Make a well in the center of the mixture and drop in the egg yolks and the 3 tablespoons water. Using a wooden spoon, mix the yolks and water. Slowly incorporate the cornstarch mixture and mix well to make a smooth thick batter. Set aside for 20 minutes.

Make the sauce: Combine the vinegar, brown sugar, tomato purée, soy sauce, peanut oil, salt and sherry in a small saucepan. Bring to a boil over moderate heat, stirring constantly. Reduce heat to low. Mix the cornstarch with the ½ cup cold water and stir the mixture into the sauce. Cook, stirring constantly, for 1 minute, until the sauce is thick and translucent. Remove pan from heat and set aside.

Preheat the oven to 250°F. Line a baking sheet with paper towels. Beat the egg whites with a whisk or rotary beater until they form stiff peaks. Fold the egg whites into the batter. Heat the oil in a deep-fryer to 375°F. Holding a shrimp by the tail, dip it into the batter, then drop carefully into the hot oil. Fry, a few at a time, for 3 to 4 minutes, until they are golden brown. Turn at least once during cooking. Using a slotted spoon, remove shrimps from the oil and drain on paper towels. Keep warm while frying the rest.

Place shrimps on a warmed serving platter and garnish with lemon wedges. Reheat the sauce, then pour it into individual bowls. Serve shrimps immediately, with the sauce.

Shellfish and Potato Croquettes

6 portions

2	cups shucked fresh oysters or shelled shrimps
4	thin scallions
1	large egg
2	cups leftover mashed potatoes

	salt and freshly ground white pepper
	flour
	Anglaise Coating
16	saltines, or 4 to 5 slices of stale bread
	oil for deep-frying

Pick over the oysters and remove any bits of shell. Drain and pat dry with paper towels. Or rinse the shrimps and pat dry. Chop oysters or shrimps in a food processor, or put through a food grinder. If using oysters, drain in a sieve. Put the shellfish in a bowl. Wash and trim scallions and mince. Beat the egg. Add minced scallions, mashed potatoes and beaten egg to the shellfish. Mix well. Taste, and add salt and white pepper as needed. Cover lightly and chill the croquette mixture for 1 hour.

Place either the saltines (for oysters) or bread (for shrimps) in a blender or a food processor and reduce to crumbs. You should have about 1½ cups. On a floured board shape the chilled shellfish mixture into 12 cork-shaped croquettes or flattened balls. Put the crumbs in a shallow bowl. Brush croquettes with the anglaise coating, then roll them in the crumbs. Lightly cover croquettes and chill for at least 1 hour. Remove from refrigerator ½ hour before frying.

Preheat oven to 250°F and line a baking sheet with paper towels. Heat the oil in a deep-fryer to 375°F. Put 6 croquettes at a time in the frying basket and fry for 4 to 5 minutes, until brown and crisp. Turn at least once during cooking. As they are finished, remove them to the baking sheet and keep warm in oven until all the croquettes are fried. Serve immediately.

Fried Chicken with Corn Fritters and Fried Bananas

4 portions

4	chicken quarters from fryers
½	cup all-purpose flour
½	teaspoon salt
¼	teaspoon freshly ground pepper
1	lemon
1	large egg
3	to 4 slices of fresh white bread
	oil for deep-frying

Corn Fritters

1	cup all-purpose flour
	pinch of salt
1	large egg
⅔	cup milk
1	cup corn kernels, fresh, frozen or canned

Fried Bananas

4	bananas
6	tablespoons butter

Halve the chicken quarters. Combine flour, salt and pepper. Grate the lemon rind to measure 1 tablespoon. Add rind to the seasoned flour and place mixture in a plastic bag. Add the chicken pieces, one at a time, and shake until coated. Beat the egg in a shallow bowl. Whirl bread in the blender until reduced to fine crumbs. You should have about 2 cups crumbs. Place the bread crumbs in another plastic bag. Dip the floured chicken pieces into the egg, then, one or two pieces at a time, place the chicken in the bag and shake in the crumbs. Repeat process to double-coat the chicken. Lay the chicken pieces in a single layer and chill for at least 2 hours. Remove and leave at room temperature for ½ hour before frying.

While the chicken is chilling, prepare the corn fritters. Sift flour and salt into a bowl. Make a well in the center and break the egg into the well. Add a little of the milk and work the flour in from the sides. Gradually add the rest of the milk to make a smooth, thick batter. Stir the corn kernels into the batter. Set aside.

Preheat oven to 250°F and line a baking sheet with paper towels. Heat oil in a deep-fryer to 360°F. Fry the chicken pieces, two at a time, for 12 to 15 minutes, until the juices run clear when the chicken is pierced with a thin skewer. Turn at least once during cooking. Test to be sure it is done to your taste. Lay the chicken pieces on the baking sheet and place them in the oven while making the fritters.

Increase the heat of the frying oil to 375°F. Drop the fritter batter by tablespoonfuls or in larger amounts into the oil and fry for 3 or 4 minutes or until the fritters are golden and puffy. As they are finished, place them on the baking sheet in the oven.

Peel bananas and halve them lengthwise and crosswise. Melt the butter in a skillet and sauté the banana pieces over moderate heat for 3 minutes, turning them with a spatula after 1½ minutes. The bananas should be golden brown; do not overcook them or they will fall apart. Serve the chicken with the fritters and bananas.

Fried Oysters

For a luncheon or supper main dish, serve these oysters with a hot sauce of shallots, cracked black pepper and red-wine vinegar, or melted butter with capers and lemon juice. Accompany with a spinach and tomato salad. The oysters can also be served as an hors d'oeuvre.

2 portions as a main course, 4 as an hors d'oeuvre

16	medium oysters
6	slices of firm white bread
1	teaspoon salt
½	teaspoon white pepper

½	teaspoon ground mace
2	large eggs
2	tablespoons water
	oil for deep-frying

Shuck the oysters, reserving the liquor (or buy them shucked at the market). Put them in an enamelware saucepan with the liquor and bring to a boil. At once pour off the liquor and spread the oysters out on a thick layer of paper towels to drain thoroughly. Check to be sure there are no bits of shell remaining.

Remove crusts from the bread slices and reduce the bread to fine crumbs in a blender or food processor. There should be about 3 cups of crumbs. Toss crumbs with the salt, pepper and mace. Beat the eggs with the water until well mixed. Pick up each oyster with tongs. Dip it into the eggs, then into the seasoned crumbs. Set them in a single layer on a plate and chill them for 1 hour.

At least 15 minutes before frying, remove oysters from

the refrigerator. Preheat the oven to 250°F and line a baking sheet with paper towels. Heat the oil in a deep-fryer to 375°F. Put half the oysters in the frying basket and fry for 3 minutes, turning once, until golden brown. As they are fried transfer them to the baking sheet and keep warm in the oven while frying the remaining oysters.

Ham and Almond Fritters

4 portions

1¼ cups water	4 eggs
8 tablespoons butter	1 pound boneless cooked ham
½ teaspoon salt	1 cup slivered blanched almonds
¼ teaspoon freshly ground pepper	oil for deep-frying
1¼ cups flour	

Pour the water into a saucepan and bring to a boil over moderate heat. Add the butter, salt and pepper. When the butter has melted, remove pan from heat and sift the flour into the pan; beat in the flour with a wooden spoon. Continue beating until the batter pulls away from the sides of the pan. Drop 1 egg into the mixture and beat until well blended before adding the next egg. When all the eggs have been absorbed, the mixture should be thick and glossy.

Remove any fat or gristle from the ham and chop or grind it. Fold the ham and almonds into the dough and set it aside to cool.

Preheat oven to 250°F and line a baking sheet with paper towels. Heat the oil in a deep-fryer to 360°F. Using a teaspoon, carefully drop heaping spoonfuls of the fritter batter into the oil. Fry the fritters for 3 to 4 minutes, or until they are golden brown. Turn at least once during cooking. With a slotted spoon, remove fritters from the oil and lay on the baking sheet. Keep fritters warm in oven while frying the rest. Serve piping hot.

Fritto Misto di Mare

(Fried Mixed Seafood)

Use at least three different kinds of fish and shellfish, preferably more, providing if possible a variety of shapes. A typical Italian mixture might include shrimps or lobsterettes (scampi), rings of squid, small whole fish and bite-size cubes of larger fish. The fish and shellfish must be very fresh, the coating light, and the frying oil hot enough to crisp and brown the coating rapidly. Fry pieces of similar size together so the time and temperature can be adjusted to suit the size.

4 portions

3	cups Fritter Batter		½	teaspoon freshly ground pepper
24	fresh shrimps in shells			oil for deep-frying
8	small whole fish, such as sardines, smelts or sprats			lemon wedges
				orange wedges
12	ounces fillets of flounder or other flat fish			parsley sprigs
12	ounces thick fillets of cod, haddock or hake		½	recipe Tomato Sauce (see Volume 4 Index)
½	cup all-purpose flour		1½	tablespoons capers
½	teaspoon salt		½	teaspoon hot red pepper flakes

Make the batter but do not add the egg whites. Chill it. Shell and devein the shrimps. Scale and gut the small whole fish if fishmonger has not done it. Cut thin fillets into 1-inch-wide diagonal strips. Remove any skin from thick fillets and cut them into 1-inch cubes. Combine the flour, salt and pepper. Toss each variety of fish separately in the seasoned flour and shake in a sieve to remove any excess. Arrange the fish in separate piles according to size. Preheat oven to 250°F. Cover a baking sheet with paper towels.

Beat the egg whites until stiff but not dry and fold them into the chilled batter until well mixed. Heat the oil in a deep-fryer to 375°F. Spear the pieces of fish on the end of a skewer, dip them into the batter, and transfer to the hot oil. Fry each batch separately by size. Small pieces will need 1 to 2 minutes, larger pieces 3 minutes. Turn once during cooking. Before adding the next batch of fish be sure the oil has regained the correct temperature. As it is done, place the seafood on the baking sheet; keep warm in the oven until ready to serve.

Reheat the tomato sauce, if necessary. Stir in the capers and, if desired, the hot red pepper flakes. Line a warmed serving dish with a paper doily and pile the fish on it, in groups. Garnish with lemon and orange wedges and parsley sprigs. Serve the sauce alongside.

Fish Croquettes

4 portions

1	small onion		½	teaspoon red pepper flakes
1	cup milk		12	ounces boneless cooked fish (cod or haddock)
2	bay leaves			
3	tablespoons butter		2	eggs
3	tablespoons flour		2	tablespoons minced fresh parsley
½	teaspoon salt			
½	teaspoon freshly ground black pepper		4	to 5 slices of stale bread
				oil for deep-frying

Peel the onion and mince to measure 3 tablespoons. Set aside. Scald the milk with the bay leaves over moderate heat by bringing it to just below a boil. Remove pan from heat and cool the milk to lukewarm. Strain the milk. In another saucepan, melt the butter over moderate heat. With a wooden spoon, stir in the flour to make a smooth paste, and cook, stirring, for 2 minutes. Remove from heat and gradually add the scalded milk, stirring constantly. Add the onion, salt, black pepper and red pepper flakes; stir to blend well. Return pan to heat and cook, stirring constantly, until sauce comes to a boil. Reduce heat to low and simmer for 3 minutes. Flake the fish and stir it into the sauce. Beat 1 egg and add to the fish mixture. Stir in the parsley and mix well. Pour the mixture into a shallow bowl, cool it, then cover lightly and chill in the refrigerator for 1 hour, until completely cold.

Place the bread in a blender or food processor and reduce to fine crumbs. You should have about 1⅓ cups. Remove fish mixture from refrigerator. With floured hands, divide the mixture into 8 to 12 equal portions and roll and shape them into croquettes. Beat remaining egg in a shallow bowl. Put the bread crumbs on a plate. Dip the croquettes into the egg, then roll them in the bread crumbs. Cover lightly and place in the refrigerator to chill for at least 1 hour. Remove from refrigerator ½ hour before frying.

Preheat the oven to 250°F and line a baking sheet with paper towels. Heat the oil in a deep-fryer to 375°F. Place the croquettes, a few at a time, in the frying basket and lower into the oil. Fry for 5 to 6 minutes or until croquettes are crisp and brown. Turn at least once during cooking. Place croquettes on a baking sheet and keep warm in oven until all are fried. Serve piping hot.

Fish and Chips

Be sure to fry the potatoes (chips) first. The longer the fish has to wait, the more the batter will soften and the fish become soggy.

6 portions

2	cups Fritter Batter		½	teaspoon freshly ground pepper
2½	pounds fish fillets (cod, haddock, hake, shark)		2½	pounds potatoes
¾	cup all-purpose flour			oil for deep-frying
¾	teaspoon salt			lemon wedges

Make the fritter batter but do not add the egg whites. Chill it. Cut the fish into pieces about 3 by 5 inches. Combine the flour, salt and pepper. Coat the pieces lightly with the seasoned flour and shake to remove any excess. Peel the potatoes and cut lengthwise into strips ½ inch wide and ½ inch thick. Dry potatoes thoroughly. Preheat the oven to 250°F and have ready two baking sheets lined with paper towels.

Heat the oil in a deep-fryer to 375°F. Divide the potatoes into sixths. One batch at a time, place them in the frying basket and lower the basket slowly into the hot oil. Fry the potatoes until golden all over and tender inside. Test one to be sure. As each batch of potatoes is fried, transfer it to one of the baking sheets and keep warm in the oven.

Finish the batter by beating the 2 egg whites until stiff but not dry and folding them into the batter. Place the bowl of batter near the deep-fryer. Reheat the oil to 375°F. Submerge a piece of fish in the batter, lift it out with a skewer, let drain briefly over the bowl, and lower gently into the hot oil. Repeat with the other pieces of fish, but fry only two or three pieces at a time. Fry the fish 3 to 5 minutes, depending on the thickness, or until the batter is crisp and golden and the fish cooked through. Turn at least once during cooking. Lift out pieces of fish with a skewer or slotted spoon and transfer to the second baking sheet. Keep the fish in the oven along with the chips until all the pieces of fish are done.

Pile the fish in the center of a large platter and surround with the chips. Garnish with lemon wedges and serve with tartar sauce or a shaker of malt vinegar.

Fish Balls with Almonds

4 portions

8	ounces fresh cod fillets		¼	teaspoon dried orégano
8	ounces smoked haddock		1	teaspoon snipped fresh chives
1	onion		2	egg yolks
½	green bell pepper		3	tablespoons milk
2	large slices of white bread		2	tablespoons flour
1	tablespoon butter		1	cup blanched almonds
½	teaspoon salt		1	whole egg
¼	teaspoon freshly ground black pepper			oil for deep-frying
1	teaspoon paprika		2	cups Tomato Sauce (see Volume 4 Index)
¼	teaspoon cayenne pepper			

Poach the cod and haddock separately until just tender (see poaching instructions in Volume 3). Drain and cool the fish, then remove any bones and skin and flake the flesh. Peel and mince the onion. Wash the pepper, discard stem, seeds and ribs, and mince. Remove crusts from bread slices and crumble the bread.

Melt the butter in a small saucepan over moderate heat. Add the onion and green pepper and sauté, stirring occasionally, for 5 minutes, or until the onion is soft and translu-cent but not browned. Transfer the vegetables to a mixing bowl. Stir in the flaked fish, crumbled bread, salt, black pepper, paprika, cayenne, orégano and chives. Beat egg yolks and milk together and add to the fish mixture. Add the flour and mix well with a spoon or your hands. The mixture should be thick enough to form into balls. With floured hands, roll the mixture into about 22 small balls, approximately 1 inch in diameter. Chop the almonds, by hand or in a nut grinder, and place them in a shallow bowl. Beat the whole egg in another shallow bowl. Roll the fish balls first in the beaten egg, then in the chopped almonds. Shake off any loose almonds and put the balls in a single layer on a plate. Cover loosely, and chill them for 1 hour. At least 15 minutes before frying, remove them from the refrigerator.

Preheat the oven to 250°F. Line a baking sheet with paper towels. Heat the oil in a deep-fryer to 375°F. Put the fish balls, about five at a time, in the frying basket and fry them for 4 to 6 minutes or until golden brown on all sides. Turn at least once during cooking. Remove them to the baking sheet and keep warm in the oven. While you are frying heat the tomato sauce. When all the fish balls are fried, transfer them to a heated serving dish. Pour the tomato sauce over them and serve immediately.

Part Three

QUICK BREADS, BISCUITS AND MUFFINS

"Give me, for a beautiful sight, a neat and smart woman, heating her oven and setting her bread! And if the bustle does not make the sign of labor glisten on her brow, where is the man that would not kiss that off, rather than lick the plaster from the cheek of a duchess?"

William Cobbett
Cottage Economy, 1832

Before the middle of the 1800s, when baking powder was invented, most leavened breads were leavened with yeast. But with the introduction of commercial baking powder a whole new world of quickly baked breads and cakes opened up for the home baker.

Today every cook should have a basic repertory of quick breads, for there is nothing that can better cheer up a humdrum meal than a warm, freshly baked loaf of homemade bread, and quick breads make such cheer possible even when time is at a premium. Because they are so easy to make, quick breads may be less exciting for the baker to produce than more elaborate yeast breads, but they are nonetheless delicious, versatile and unfailingly popular. Almost all quick breads can be prepared from start to finish in an hour, and many require far less than that.

Soda bread is the traditional bread of Ireland and is still baked daily in farmhouses and city kitchens all over that country. It is said that every woman has her own treasured recipe that has been handed down from generation to generation. In some remote country areas, Irish soda bread is still baked in a *bastable oven*—a footed iron pot that is similar to the American cast-iron spider skillet. It has a lid, handles and three short legs, and is used for cooking over an open fire. When soda bread is baked this way, the lid of the oven is covered with hot glowing embers to insure even heat. Cooked in this fashion this bread is called a *bastable cake*.

Soda bread may be made with white or whole-wheat flour, but it is always leavened with baking soda; buttermilk or soured milk is used for mixing. An Irish cook always takes care to stir the ingredients in a clockwise direction when mixing a dough for soda bread as this is said to placate Druid ancestors. A cross is slashed across the unbaked loaf to let the devil out (and, not incidentally, to allow the loaf to expand as it bakes).

"Everybody who cooks," writes Elizabeth David, "in however limited a way, should know how to make a loaf of soda bread. Rapidly mixed, immediately consigned to the oven or the griddle, the demands of this kind of dough are the very reverse of those made by yeast-leavened bread doughs. High-speed action rather than patience, quick, light handling instead of hard kneading and tough treatment, are necessary when it comes to baking powder doughs. And if, after all possible care has been taken, your soda bread still seems rather more like cake than bread in texture and in the way it cuts, that is what soda bread is called in most parts of Ireland—cake or 'cake of bread', whereas a loaf of bread is one bought from the bakery." (*English Bread and Yeast Cookery*)

A scone, or skon, pronounced to rhyme with John, is a small Scottish cousin of the Irish soda bread. Originally scones were always baked on a griddle (called a girdle in Scotland), but today they are more often baked in the oven. They may be made from wheat, barley, oatmeal or potato flour, and although there are hundreds of variations on the basic recipe, scones are always quickly and simply made and are traditional teatime fare accompanied by jam, butter, cream and honey.

American cooks have produced a large variety of quick breads—including an astonishing number of recipes for corn bread, innumerable muffins, biscuits and cakelike loaves of tea bread studded with fruit and nuts.

The early colonists learned about corn and corn meal from the Indians and, because wheat flour was scarce, quickly learned to use corn meal along with regular flour in making bread. ". . . And gradually," writes Evan Jones in *American Food,* "one good recipe followed another—from the most primitive ash cakes to hoecakes to corn pones to corn sticks to Johnny cake to hush puppies. . . ." By the time Benjamin Franklin was representing the colonies in London in 1768, corn breads and cakes were such familiar and beloved fare that he had his wife send packages of corn meal across the ocean and Mr. Franklin himself taught his English cook how to prepare the various corn breads that he loved so well. "Pray let me, an American, affirm that Indian corn, take it all in all, is one of the most agreeable and wholesome grains in the world . . . and that johnny or hoecake, hot from the fire, is better than a Yorkshire muffin . . ." wrote Benjamin Franklin in a letter to the *London Gazetteer.*

If William Cobbett's sentiment, "Without bread, all is misery," is true, then the quick bread recipes in the following pages should insure that with a minimum of time, fuss and bother you need never serve a breadless meal again.

QUICK BREADS

Quick breads, leavened with baking powder or baking soda, are a delicious alternative to those made with yeast. Easy and fast to prepare and extremely versatile, the breads may be plain, sweet or savory. Some, like tea breads and muffins, are moist and cakelike; others, biscuits and scones, for example, are flaky or somewhat dry and crumbly. Despite these wide variations in flavor and texture, all quick breads fall into one of two categories: dough breads, which include soda bread, biscuits and scones; and batter breads, such as corn bread, tea breads and muffins.

Ingredients for Quick Bread

Flour and Other Grains. All-purpose flour is the basic flour used in quick breads. Whole-wheat flour, which produces a close-textured bread with a nutty flavor, is not sifted, as is all-purpose flour, because sifting would remove the bran. Whole-wheat quick breads that contain dried fruit, nuts, spices, cheese or herbs are particularly successful.

Corn meal is essential in making corn bread. Although yellow corn meal is specified in our recipes, white corn meal will also do.

Rolled oats added to quick breads contribute an earthy flavor and interesting texture as well as considerable nutritional benefits.

Leaveners. The two chemical leaveners used in making quick breads are baking powder and baking soda (bicarbonate of soda). Depending on the other ingredients, they may be used singly or together. When they are mixed with liquid, these leaveners produce carbon dioxide, which causes the dough or batter to rise.

Baking powder reacts in two stages: the first, when it is combined with the liquid in the dough; the second, when it is heated during baking. Baking soda is activated when it is combined with an acidic ingredient, such as buttermilk, sour cream, yogurt or molasses. Breads leavened with baking soda should be placed in the oven soon after they are shaped or the leavening power of the soda may be exhausted before the bread is baked.

Fats. Butter, margarine, lard, vegetable shortening and occasionally oils are used in quick breads to enrich the dough and improve the texture. The more fat incorporated, the richer and softer the loaf will be and the longer it will keep.

Eggs. Eggs enhance the flavor, color and texture of a quick bread, and they also act as a leavener. When eggs are beaten, air is trapped in their protein. The protein expands and then sets during baking, which helps the bread first to rise and then to stay risen.

Sweeteners. Granulated and brown sugar as well as liquid sweeteners, such as molasses, honey and syrups, may be added to quick breads for flavor and texture. The sharp edges of granulated sugar crystals help to trap air, which causes the bread to rise. Brown sugar is used for its deeper flavor and rich color and is often added to whole-wheat breads. Because they are so dense, liquid sweeteners are often used in breads intended to have a close, heavy texture.

Liquids. Milk, buttermilk, sour cream and yogurt are the liquids most frequently called for, although puréed fruit or vegetables are sometimes used.

Flavorings. Be creative with these, using them to change old familiar recipes or develop new ones. Dried fruit is added to many quick breads for flavor and texture. Currants, raisins and dates are most often used, but any other dried fruit, pitted and chopped, if necessary, is also suitable. For dough breads, dried fruit is stirred into the dry ingredients before liquid is added; for batter breads, the fruit is added to the finished batter.

Glacé fruits (such as cherries, citron, pineapple), candied angelica and crystallized ginger make attractive additions to a tea bread. For example, crystallized ginger would be a delicious addition to the Jamaican Spice Loaf (omit the ground ginger). Chop the fruit to the size required and then toss it lightly in a small amount of flour to prevent it from sinking to the bottom of the batter.

Fresh fruit may be added to sweetened breads. Peel and core or pit the fruit and cut it to the required size. Small berries may be left whole. Fold the fruit into the finished mixture.

Grated citrus rind, stirred in along with the liquid, adds subtle flavor and freshness.

Seeds and chopped nuts, either toasted or raw, may be stirred into the dry ingredients or folded into the finished mixture.

Ground spices, sifted in with the dry ingredients, are effective flavorings, used alone or to bring out the flavor of other ingredients, especially fruit. Grind whole spices whenever possible and do not use a spice that has been sitting on the shelf for too long; it will have lost its flavor.

Chopped fresh or dried herbs add zest to unsweetened quick breads. Stir them into the sifted dry ingredients.

Freshly ground pepper, dry mustard, cayenne and other seasonings may be added to savory breads according to taste. Salt is used in all quick breads, savory and sweet, to bring out flavor.

Grated cheese is a delicious addition to savory breads, and it helps to produce a tender texture as well. Use a flavorful high-quality grating cheese, such as Cheddar or Parmesan.

Other savory ingredients might include chopped sautéed onions or garlic or other cooked or raw vegetables, as long as they are not too liquid or acidic.

Equipment

A reliable oven is the most important piece of equipment you will need in baking. Otherwise, very little special equipment is required for making quick breads.

Basic Baking Powder Bread

one ¾-pound loaf

2	cups all-purpose flour
4	teaspoons baking powder
1	teaspoon salt
½.	cup milk
1	teaspoon lemon juice
	cracked wheat or poppy seeds

1 Preheat oven to 425°F. Sprinkle a baking sheet with extra flour to cover evenly.

2 Sift flour, baking powder, and salt into a bowl. Make a well in the center of the ingredients.

3 Reserve 2 teaspoons of the milk. Pour remainder plus lemon juice into dry ingredients.

4 Using a fork or round-bladed knife, mix the liquid into the flour until the dough clings together.

5 Turn the mixture out on a lightly floured surface and knead briefly until the dough is smooth.

6 Using your hands, shape the dough into a round and place on the prepared baking sheet.

7 Brush the dough with the reserved milk. Sprinkle lightly with cracked wheat or poppy seeds.

8 Bake on the center shelf of the oven for 25 to 30 minutes, or until well risen and golden brown.

Basic Scones

Makes about 12 scones

2 cups all-purpose flour
1 tablespoon baking powder
½ teaspoon salt
4 tablespoons unsalted
    butter, chilled
½ cup milk
    milk for glazing

1 Preheat oven to 425°F. Set rack in center of oven. Sift flour, baking powder and salt into a mixing bowl.

2 Work fat into flour with pastry blender, two table knives or your fingertips until mixture resembles coarse meal.

3 Make well in center of mixture, pour in all but 2 tablespoons of the milk, and stir to make a soft dough, adding remaining milk if necessary.

4 Gather the dough together with your fingers and turn out onto a lightly floured board.

5 Knead lightly and quickly until the dough is smooth and free of cracks.

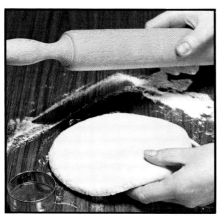

6 Roll out to a ½-inch-thick round, turning dough 45° to your left after each stroke.

7 Using a floured 2-inch biscuit cutter, stamp out scones. Press cutter down firmly and sharply; do not twist.

8 Place scones on baking sheet, 1 inch apart. Brush with milk for glazing and bake for 12 to 15 minutes. Serve warm.

Irish Soda Bread

one 2-pound loaf

6 cups all-purpose flour
1 teaspoon salt
2 teaspoons baking soda, or
   1 teaspoon baking soda
   plus 1 teaspoon cream
   of tartar

5 teaspoons unsalted butter
   or lard, chilled
1 cup buttermilk
   milk for glazing

1 Preheat the oven to 400°F. Sift flour, salt and baking soda into a mixing bowl. Flour a large baking sheet.

2 Using a pastry blender, two table knives, or your fingertips, work fat into flour until mixture resembles coarse meal.

3 Make a well in the center of the flour mixture and pour in the buttermilk.

4 Draw the mixture into the liquid using a fork or round-bladed knife until the dough forms fairly large lumps.

5 Using your fingertips, lightly press the mixture together and draw the dough into a ball. Turn out and knead about 1 minute.

6 Place the dough on a baking sheet and shape into a round loaf about 8 inches in diameter and 1½ inches thick.

7 Using a sharp, floured knife, cut a deep cross on the top of the dough and then brush the top of the dough with milk.

8 Bake on the upper shelf of the oven for 30 to 35 minutes, until bread is risen and golden brown.

9 Remove the loaf from the oven and transfer to a wire rack to cool for at least 15 minutes before eating.

A pastry blender is useful but not necessary for mixing dough breads. Two table knives or your fingers will do. To cut biscuits, you should have a 2-inch biscuit cutter, but the rim of a thin glass is a fine substitute.

Use standard loaf pans, 8 or 9 inches; a large baking sheet is used for free-form loaves, biscuits and scones. Square baking pans, 8 or 9 inches, are required for some coffee cakes and quick breads, and regular (3½-ounce capacity) muffin tins for muffin recipes. If you do not have a pan of the particular size specified in the recipe, use a larger size rather than a smaller one; this will keep batter from spilling onto the oven floor. (If a larger pan is used, the baking time may have to be reduced slightly.)

Making Quick Breads

Preparation. Preheat the oven to the temperature specified in the recipe and set the rack in the center of the oven. If you are going to use two baking sheets, place one in the middle level of the oven and the other in the upper third. Butter or coat the pans as required.

Mixing Dough Quick Breads. This method is similar to that for making short-crust pie pastry (see Volume 2 Index). Measure the dry ingredients and sift them into a mixing bowl. Cut the chilled fat into small pieces and distribute them over the dry ingredients. Using a pastry blender, two table knives, or your fingertips, work the fat into the flour until the mixture is crumbly and resembles coarse meal. Stir in sugar and dry flavorings, using a fork to keep the mixture light and aerated. To add the liquid, make a well in the center of the flour mixture and pour in almost all the liquid. Still using a fork, quickly mix in the dry ingredients until a soft dough is formed. If the dough seems stiff, add the remaining liquid. It is important to work the ingredients lightly and quickly, as overmixing will toughen the bread.

Scoop out the dough onto a light-ly floured surface and knead it for less than 1 minute, giving it 6 to 8 turns, until it is smooth. Shape the dough as directed in the recipe.

All the dough quick breads in this section have been written for the hand-mixing method, which is very easy and gives you more control of the dough. If you wish to use an electric mixer or food processor, do it according to the following instructions. For an electric mixer, place the fat, sugar, eggs, other liquids and flavorings in the large bowl of the mixer. Sift the dry ingredients over them. Using the paddle or beaters, mix on lowest speed for about 20 seconds, then stop and scrape down the bowl with a plastic or rubber spatula. Mix at low speed again for about 15 seconds, or until the ingredients are combined. Do not overmix. The dough is now ready to be shaped. For a food processor, place the butter, sugar, eggs, other liquids and flavorings in the bowl of the processor with the steel blade in place. Add all the dry ingredients. Pulse about 10 times, or just until the dough is mixed. Scrape down the sides of the bowl and pulse 10 times more. Shape the dough as directed.

Mixing Batter Quick Breads. The dry ingredients are usually sifted into a mixing bowl and the liquid is stirred in quickly just until the ingredients are well moistened. It is important not to overmix; light rapid mixing is crucial to achieving a light texture. This is most easily accomplished by hand, but an electric mixer may be used when creaming is specified. Nuts, seeds and fruit may then be stirred in and the batter poured or spooned into the prepared pans.

Baking. If your oven has hot spots, turn the bread midway through baking so that it browns evenly. If you decide to double a recipe and are baking in two pans that fit on one rack, place them so that they do not touch. If using two racks, arrange the pans so that one is not directly underneath the other. This will allow as much heat as possible to circulate freely.

Cooling and Storing. Loaves and muffins should cool in their pans for 4 or 5 minutes before they are turned out on wire racks. Corn bread and scones are best served still warm from the oven. Biscuits should be served as soon as they are removed from the oven.

Some quick breads taste better if they have been allowed to sit overnight. Cool the bread completely on a wire rack, wrap it in plastic wrap, and store it at room temperature. To store longer, place the wrapped bread in an airtight cake tin or plastic food container. The length of storage time will be governed by the ingredients. A plain bread will store for one to three days and an enriched loaf with ingredients such as eggs, fat, fruit and sugar for just over a week. Tea breads, in particular, freeze very well. You may want to bake two loaves at a time and freeze one for unexpected company.

To freeze, wrap the bread in freezer paper or heavy-duty foil. Store in the freezer for up to four weeks. Thaw the bread in its wrapping at room temperature; it will take approximately 4 hours to thaw a 9-inch loaf. If you are in a hurry and intend to eat the bread immediately, unwrap the loaf and thaw it for 30 minutes in an oven preheated to 300°F; this method, however, is less satisfactory because it tends to dry out the bread and causes it to go stale more quickly.

Biscuits and scones should be eaten the same day they are made. Freshly baked scones, however, may be successfully frozen for up to six months. As soon as they are completely cooled, place them in heavy-duty plastic freezer bags and freeze at once. Thaw in the freezer bag at room temperature for 1 hour.

Serving. Depending on the bread and the occasion, quick breads may be served with spreads such as butter, cream cheese, jam or puréed fruit, or used to make delicate sandwiches. Leftover tea breads may be sliced and toasted for breakfast or as a snack.

Date and Walnut Bread

one 8-inch loaf

8	ounces pitted dates
2	cups all-purpose flour
2	teaspoons baking powder
1	teaspoon salt

⅔	cup dark brown sugar, packed
½	cup chopped walnuts
1	large egg
⅔	cup milk

Preheat the oven to 350°F. Lightly butter an 8-inch loaf pan.

Chop the dates into small pieces. Sift the flour, baking powder and salt into a mixing bowl. Add the sugar, dates and walnuts and stir until well combined. Combine the egg and the milk in a small bowl and beat lightly with a wire whisk. Using a wooden spoon, stir the liquid into the flour mixture just until the ingredients are well moistened. Do not overmix. Pour the batter into the prepared loaf pan.

Place the bread in the oven and bake for 1 to 1½ hours, or until a skewer inserted into the center of the loaf comes out clean. Remove the loaf from the oven and allow it to cool in the pan for 5 minutes. Invert the loaf onto a wire rack and cool completely before serving.

Variation: Substitute 2 cups of unsifted whole-wheat flour for the all-purpose flour. Increase the baking powder to a total of 2½ teaspoons and sift it together with ¼ teaspoon ground allspice and the salt into a mixing bowl. Stir in the unsifted whole-wheat flour, and continue with the recipe.

Raisin Loaf

one 9-inch loaf

4 tablespoons plus 1 teaspoon unsalted butter	1 cup raisins
1 cup sugar	2 cups all-purpose flour
1 cup milk	1 tablespoon baking powder
	1 large egg

Preheat the oven to 350°F. Lightly coat a 9-inch loaf pan with the 1 teaspoon of butter.

Cut the 4 tablespoons of butter into pieces and place in a 3-quart saucepan. Add the sugar, milk and raisins and place the pan over moderate heat. Gradually bring the mixture to a boil, stirring occasionally. Remove the pan from the heat and set aside. Sift the flour with the baking powder. When the milk mixture has cooled, add the flour, ¼ cup at a time, stirring until it is incorporated. Beat the egg lightly, add to the ingredients in the pan, and beat until thoroughly mixed. Spoon the batter into the prepared loaf pan.

Bake the raisin loaf for 1¼ hours, or until a skewer inserted into the center comes out clean. Remove the loaf from the oven and let it cool in the pan for 10 minutes. Invert the loaf onto a wire rack to cool completely before serving.

Whole-Wheat Bread with Fruit and Cheese Topping

one 9-inch square

10	tablespoons plus 2 teaspoons unsalted butter, chilled		¾	cup light brown sugar, packed
2	teaspoons baking powder		1	medium-size egg
½	teaspoon salt		2	medium-size apples
2	cups whole-wheat flour		2	medium-size bananas
			8	ounces cottage cheese

Preheat the oven to 400°F. Coat a 9-inch square baking pan with the 2 teaspoons of butter.

Sift the baking powder and salt into a mixing bowl. Add the flour and stir with a fork until well combined. Cut 8 tablespoons of the butter into small pieces and add to the dry ingredients. Using a pastry blender, two table knives, or your fingertips, work the fat into the flour until it resembles coarse meal of approximately uniform size. Using a fork, stir in ½ cup of the sugar until it is evenly incorporated. Beat the egg lightly. Make a well in the flour mixture and add the egg. Using a fork, stir the ingredients until the mixture begins to cling together. Using your fingers, press the dough, which should be fairly stiff, into a ball and place on a lightly floured surface. Knead briefly until the dough is smooth, approximately 1 minute. Using short, even strokes, roll the dough into a 9-inch square. Lift the dough by rolling it around the rolling pin. Carefully unroll it into the prepared pan. Press the dough with your knuckles or fingertips to fit the pan.

Peel, core, and chop the apples into ½- to ¾-inch chunks. Peel and chop the bananas. Sprinkle the apples and bananas evenly over the surface of the dough. Spread the cottage cheese over the fruit and press it down lightly with the back of a spoon. Sprinkle the remaining ¼ cup sugar over the cheese. Cut the remaining 2 tablespoons of butter into small pieces and dot the sugar with them.

Bake the bread for 25 to 30 minutes, or until the dough has risen evenly underneath the filling. Remove the pan from the oven. Allow the bread to cool for 15 minutes in the pan, then cut into squares and serve warm, or allow to cool completely before serving.

Whole-Wheat and Oat Bread

one 8-inch loaf

3	tablespoons unsalted butter, at room temperature			generous ½ cup rolled oats
2½	cups whole-wheat flour		¾	cup wheat germ
1	teaspoon baking powder		¼	cup light brown sugar, packed
½	teaspoon baking soda		⅔	cup sour cream
½	teaspoon salt		2	medium-size eggs

Preheat the oven to 400°F. Use 1 tablespoon of the butter to coat an 8-inch loaf pan.

Place the flour, baking powder, baking soda, salt, oats, wheat germ and sugar in a large mixing bowl; stir with a fork until thoroughly blended. Place the remaining 2 tablespoons butter, sour cream and eggs in another bowl, and beat until well combined. Add the liquid mixture to the dry ingredients and mix together with a wooden spoon until it forms a mass.

Turn out on a floured surface and knead about 1 minute, until the dough is smooth. Put the dough in the prepared pan and place in the oven.

Bake the bread for 30 to 35 minutes, or until the loaf is well risen and golden brown. Remove the loaf from the oven and allow the bread to cool in the pan for 5 minutes. Turn out onto a wire rack and allow to cool completely.

Variations: For an herb loaf, add 2 teaspoons of mixed dried herbs or 2 tablespoons chopped fresh herbs to the dry ingredients. For a caraway loaf, stir 1 teaspoon caraway seeds into the dry ingredients.

Banana Walnut Bread

one 9-inch loaf

¼ cup plus 1 teaspoon vegetable shortening	2 cups all-purpose flour
⅔ cup sugar	1 teaspoon baking powder
3 large eggs	¼ teaspoon baking soda
4 medium-size bananas	½ teaspoon salt
	1 cup chopped walnuts

Preheat the oven to 350°F. Coat a 9-inch loaf pan with the 1 teaspoon of shortening.

In the medium-size bowl of an electric mixer, cream the ¼ cup shortening, sugar and eggs until light. Peel the bananas and mash them in a food processor, in a ricer, or with a fork. Add the bananas to the creamed mixture and beat well. Sift the flour, baking powder, baking soda, and salt into the banana mixture and mix just until the ingredients are well moistened. Do not overmix. Stir in the walnuts. Pour the batter into the prepared loaf pan.

Bake the bread for 1 to 1¼ hours, or until the loaf is well risen and golden brown and a skewer inserted into the center of the loaf comes out clean.

Remove the pan from the oven and allow the loaf to cool in the pan for 5 minutes. Invert onto a wire rack to cool completely.

Corn Bread

one 8-inch square

5	tablespoons unsalted butter, chilled	2	teaspoons baking powder
1	cup plus 2½ tablespoons yellow corn meal	1	teaspoon salt
1	cup all-purpose flour	1	cup milk
		1	medium-size egg

Preheat the oven to 400°F. Coat an 8-inch square cake pan with 1 tablespoon of the butter.

Sift the corn meal, flour, baking powder and salt into a mixing bowl. Cut the remaining 4 tablespoons butter into small pieces and add to the dry ingredients. Using a pastry blender, two table knives, or your fingertips, work the butter into the mixture until it resembles coarse meal. Beat the milk and egg together. Make a well in the center of the flour mixture and pour in the liquid. Stir the batter with a wooden spoon just until all the ingredients are well blended. Pour the batter into the prepared pan.

Bake for 25 to 30 minutes, or until a skewer inserted into the center of the bread comes out clean. Remove the corn bread from the oven and allow to cool in the pan for 5 minutes. Invert onto a wire rack to cool, or serve warm.

Jamaican Spice Loaf

one 9-inch loaf

4	tablespoons plus 1 tea-spoon unsalted butter		½	teaspoon freshly grated nutmeg
3	cups all-purpose flour		1	teaspoon ground ginger
1½	teaspoons baking soda		½	cup raisins
½	teaspoon salt		¼	cup molasses
½	teaspoon ground allspice		3	large eggs
½	teaspoon ground cinnamon		¼	cup milk

Preheat the oven to 325°F. Coat a 9-inch loaf pan with the 1 teaspoon of butter.

Sift the flour, baking soda, salt and spices into a mixing bowl; stir in the raisins. In a small saucepan, heat the molasses and 4 tablespoons butter over moderate heat, stirring constantly. When the butter has melted into the molasses, pour the mixture into the flour mixture, stirring constantly. Break the eggs into another bowl. Add the milk and beat until blended. Pour the milk and eggs into the flour mixture, stirring until all the ingredients are combined. Pour the batter into the prepared loaf pan.

Bake Jamaican spice loaf for 1¼ hours, or until a skewer inserted into the center of the loaf comes out clean. Remove the pan from the oven and let cool for 5 minutes. Invert the loaf onto a wire rack to cool completely, then cut into slices and serve.

Finnish Bread

A plain bread with a rich flavor that should be eaten within one day of baking.

one 8-inch loaf

3	large eggs		2	cups all-purpose flour
¾	cup light cream		¼	teaspoon salt
¼	cup milk		¼	teaspoon sugar
¼	cup buttermilk			

Preheat the oven to 350°F. Generously butter an 8-inch loaf pan. Separate the eggs, placing the whites in a medium-size mixing bowl and the yolks in a smaller bowl. Add the cream, milk and buttermilk to the yolks and beat with a fork. Set aside. Sift the flour, salt and sugar into a large bowl. Make a well in the center and pour in the egg mixture. With a wooden spoon, gradually mix the dry ingredients into the liquid just until the ingredients are well moistened. Do not overmix. Set aside. With a wire whisk or rotary beater, beat the egg whites until they form stiff peaks. Using a rubber spatula, carefully fold the whites into the batter. Pour the batter into the prepared loaf pan.

Bake the bread for 1½ hours, or until the top is golden brown and a skewer inserted into the center of the loaf comes out clean. Remove the pan from the oven and allow the loaf to cool completely in the pan before turning out and serving.

Pumpkin Pecan Bread

one 9-inch loaf

4	tablespoons plus 1 teaspoon unsalted butter, at room temperature	2½	cups all-purpose flour
		1	tablespoon baking powder
¾	cup light brown sugar, packed	¼	teaspoon salt
		¼	teaspoon ground cinnamon
2	large eggs	¼	teaspoon freshly grated nutmeg
1	cup pumpkin purée*	1	cup chopped pecans

Preheat the oven to 350°F. Lightly coat a 9-inch loaf pan with the 1 teaspoon of butter.

Place the 4 tablespoons butter, sugar and eggs in the medium-size bowl of an electric mixer; cream the mixture until it is light and fluffy. Add the pumpkin purée and beat well. Sift the flour, baking powder, salt and spices over the pumpkin mixture and mix just until ingredients are well moistened. Do not overbeat. Stir in the pecans. Pour the batter into the prepared loaf pan.

Bake the bread for 1 to 1¼ hours, or until a skewer inserted into the center of the loaf comes out clean. Remove the loaf from the oven and let it cool in the pan for 10 minutes. Invert onto a wire rack to cool completely before serving.

*If you use canned pumpkin, be sure to buy plain purée and not pumpkin pie mix.

Cheese Biscuits

12 to 14 biscuits

5	tablespoons unsalted butter, chilled	1	teaspoon dry mustard
		4	teaspoons baking powder
4	ounces Chedder cheese	⅔	cup milk
2	cups all-purpose flour		milk for glazing
¼	teaspoon salt		

Preheat the oven to 450°F. Lightly coat a large baking sheet with 1 tablespoon of the butter.

Grate the cheese; you should have 1 cup. Sift the flour, salt, mustard and baking powder into a mixing bowl. Cut the remaining 4 tablespoons butter into small pieces and add to the flour mixture. Using a pastry blender, two table knives, or your fingertips, work the fat into the dry ingredients until the mixture is crumbly and resembles coarse meal. Stir in the cheese with a fork. Make a well in the center of the mixture and pour in almost all of the milk. Quickly stir the mixture with a fork to make a soft dough, adding the remaining milk if necessary. Turn the dough out onto a floured surface and knead for about 1 minute, or just until the dough is smooth. Roll out the dough to ½-inch thickness. Using a floured 2-inch biscuit cutter, cut out rounds and place them, 1 inch apart, on the prepared baking sheet. Gather the scraps into a ball, pressing them together lightly, roll out again, and cut more biscuits. Brush the tops of the biscuits with milk.

Bake for 12 to 15 minutes, or until the biscuits are golden brown. Remove from the oven and serve immediately.

Baking Powder Biscuits

12 biscuits

2	cups all-purpose flour
1	tablespoon baking powder
½	teaspoon salt

⅓	cup lard or unsalted butter, chilled
¾	cup milk, approximately
	milk for glazing

Preheat the oven to 450°F. Sift the flour, baking powder and salt into a mixing bowl. Cut the lard or butter into 4 or 5 pieces and add to the flour mixture. Using a pastry blender, two table knives, or your fingertips, work the fat into the dry ingredients until the mixture is crumbly and resembles coarse meal. Make a well in the dry ingredients and pour in the milk. With a fork, quickly stir the dry ingredients into the milk to make a soft dough, adding a little more milk if necessary. Turn the dough out onto a floured surface and knead about 1 minute, or just until the dough is smooth.

Roll out the dough to ⅓-inch thickness and cut into rounds with a floured 2-inch biscuit cutter, making the cuts close together to get as many biscuits as possible out of the first rolling. Gather the scraps of dough into a ball, pressing together lightly, roll out again, and cut out more biscuits. Place the rounds on a buttered baking sheet, setting them 1 inch apart from each other, and brush the tops with milk.

Bake the biscuits for 12 to 15 minutes. Remove from the oven and serve immediately.

Bran and Nut Muffins

12 muffins

5½	tablespoons unsalted butter
1	cup all-purpose flour
¼	cup sugar
½	teaspoon salt
2	teaspoons baking powder

¾	cup bran flakes
⅓	cup chopped nuts
1	large egg
1	cup milk

Preheat the oven to 400°F. Lightly coat a 12-cup muffin tin with 1½ tablespoons of the butter. Sift the flour, sugar, salt and baking powder into a large mixing bowl. Stir in the bran and nuts. Place the remaining 4 tablespoons butter in a small pan and set over low heat to melt. Break the egg into a small bowl and beat with a wire whisk or rotary beater until thick and light-colored. Add the milk and beat to combine. Pour the egg mixture into the dry ingredients and stir the mixture with a wooden spoon until all the ingredients are just combined but not smooth. Do not overbeat. Fold the melted butter into the batter. Turn the mixture into the prepared muffin tins.

Bake for 25 minutes, or until a skewer inserted into the center of a muffin comes out clean. Remove the muffins from the oven and let cool about 5 minutes. Turn out and serve at once or set on wire racks to cool completely.

Cheese Muffins

12 muffins

5½	tablespoons unsalted butter
2	ounces Cheddar cheese
2	cups all-purpose flour
2	teaspoons baking powder
½	teaspoon salt

⅛	teaspoon freshly ground pepper
2	large eggs
⅔	cup milk

Preheat the oven to 450°F. Generously coat a 12-cup muffin tin with 1½ tablespoons of the butter. Grate the cheese; you should have ½ cup.

Sift the flour, baking powder, salt and pepper into a large mixing bowl. Place the remaining 4 tablespoons butter in a small pan and set over low heat to melt. Break the eggs into a smaller bowl and beat with a wire whisk or rotary beater until they are thick and light-colored and fall in a steady ribbon from the whisk. Add the milk and melted butter to the eggs and stir well. Stir the egg mixture into the dry ingredients as quickly as possible. Do not overbeat; the ingredients should be just combined but not smooth. Stir in the grated cheese. Spoon the batter into the prepared muffin tins and bake for 15 to 20 minutes, or until a skewer inserted into one of the muffins comes out clean. Remove the muffins from the oven and cool in the pan for about 5 minutes. Turn the muffins out and serve warm, or set on wire racks to cool completely.

Apple Muffins

12 muffins

5½	tablespoons unsalted butter
1	lemon
2	cups all-purpose flour
½	teaspoon salt
2	teaspoons baking powder
¼	cup sugar
½	teaspoon ground cinnamon
¼	teaspoon freshly grated nutmeg
¼	teaspoon ground allspice
2	large eggs
⅔	cup buttermilk
2	medium-size apples

Preheat the oven to 450°F. Coat a 12-cup muffin tin with 1½ tablespoons of the butter and set aside.

Squeeze the lemon to measure 1 tablespoon juice. Sift the flour, salt, baking powder, sugar and spices into a large mixing bowl. Set the remaining 4 tablespoons butter to melt over low heat. Break the eggs into a bowl and beat with a wire whisk or rotary beater until the eggs are thick and light-colored and fall in a steady ribbon from the whisk. Add the melted butter, buttermilk and lemon juice. Peel, core and grate the apples. Stir the egg mixture into the dry ingredients as quickly as possible. Do not overbeat; the ingredients should be just combined but not smooth. Fold in the grated apple. Spoon the batter into the prepared muffin tins.

Place the tins in the center of the oven and bake the muffins for 15 to 20 minutes, or until a skewer inserted into the center of a muffin comes out clean. Remove from the oven and allow them to cool in the pan for about 5 minutes. Turn them out and serve at once, or allow the muffins to cool completely on wire racks.

Raisin Scones

6 wedges

5	tablespoons unsalted butter, chilled		2	tablespoons sugar
2	cups all-purpose flour		⅓	cup raisins
1	tablespoon baking powder		½	cup milk
½	teaspoon salt		1	tablespoon honey

Preheat the oven to 425°F. Lightly coat a baking sheet with 1 tablespoon of the butter. Sift the flour, baking powder and salt into a mixing bowl. Cut the remaining 4 tablespoons butter into small pieces and add to the flour. Using a pastry blender, two table knives, or your fingertips, work the fat into the flour until the mixture is crumbly and resembles coarse meal. Add the sugar and raisins and stir with a fork until well combined. Make a well in the dry ingredients and pour in all but 2 tablespoons of the milk. With a fork, quickly stir the dry ingredients into the milk to make a soft dough, adding the remaining milk if necessary. Turn the dough out onto a lightly floured surface and knead about 1 minute, or just until smooth. Shape the dough into a round and press out lightly until it is ½ inch thick. Place the round on the prepared baking sheet. Flour the blade of a sharp knife and score the round into 6 wedges, cutting deeply into the dough but not through to the bottom. Brush the surface of the dough with the honey.

Bake the scones for 20 to 25 minutes, or until they have risen and are a golden color. Remove the round from the oven and place on a heated serving dish. Separate into wedges and serve at once, or place wedges on wire racks to cool completely.

Blueberry Muffins

18 muffins

10	tablespoons unsalted butter		1½	teaspoons salt
3½	cups plus 2 tablespoons all-purpose flour		¾	cup sugar
10	ounces fresh or defrosted frozen unsweetened blueberries		4	teaspoons baking powder
			4	large eggs
			1½	cups milk

Preheat the oven to 450°F. Coat 18 muffin cups with 2 tablespoons of the butter and sprinkle them lightly with 1 tablespoon of the flour. Tip and rotate to distribute the flour evenly and shake out the excess. Set aside.

If you are using fresh blueberries, hull, wash, and thoroughly drain the fruit. Spread out the fresh or defrosted berries on a sheet of wax paper, gently pat dry with paper towels and sprinkle them with another tablespoon of flour. Set aside.

Place the remaining 8 tablespoons of butter over low heat to melt. In a medium-size mixing bowl, sift together the remaining 3½ cups flour, salt, sugar and baking powder. In another bowl, beat the eggs with a wire whisk or rotary beater until they are thick and light-colored. Add the melted butter and milk to the egg mixture and stir with a wooden spoon. Stir the egg mixture into the flour, as quickly as possible. Do not overbeat; the ingredients should be just combined, but not smooth. Fold the blueberries into the batter.

Spoon the batter into the prepared muffin tins. Bake about 15 minutes, or until a skewer inserted into the center of a muffin comes out clean. Remove the muffins from the oven and allow them to cool in the tins for about 5 minutes. Turn out and serve at once or place on racks to cool completely.

Whole-Wheat Scones with Herbs

6 wedges

1	teaspoon baking soda		4	tablespoons unsalted butter, chilled
1	teaspoon cream of tartar		1	teaspoon mixed dried herbs
½	teaspoon salt		½	cup plain yogurt
	large pinch of freshly ground pepper			milk for glazing
2	cups whole-wheat flour			

Preheat the oven to 425°F. Sift the baking soda, cream of tartar, salt and pepper into a mixing bowl. Add the flour and stir with a fork until the ingredients are well combined. Cut the butter into small pieces and add to the flour mixture. Using a pastry blender, two table knives, or your fingertips, work the fat into the dry ingredients until the mixture is crumbly and resembles coarse meal. Stir in the herbs. Make a well in the center of the mixture and spoon in all but 2 tablespoons of the yogurt. With a fork, stir the flour mixture into the yogurt to make a soft dough, adding the remaining yogurt if necessary. Turn the dough out onto a lightly floured surface and knead for about 1 minute, or just until the dough is smooth. Shape the dough into a round and press lightly until it is ½ inch thick. Place the round on a baking sheet. Flour the blade of a sharp knife and score the round into six wedges, cutting deeply into the dough but not through to the bottom. Brush the surface of the dough with milk.

Bake the scones for 20 to 25 minutes, or until they have risen and are a pale gold. Remove the round from the oven and transfer to a heated serving dish. Separate into wedges and serve at once, or place wedges on wire racks to cool completely.

Part Four
MERINGUES

Humpty Dumpty sat on a wall,
Humpty Dumpty had a great fall.
 All the king's horses
 And all the king's men
Couldn't put Humpty together again.

Nursery rhyme

English-speaking children chant about Humpty Dumpty. In other countries children recite similar rhymes about Humpelken-Pumpelken, Runtzelken-Puntzelken, Wirgele-Wargele, Gigele-Gagele, Lille-Trille, Annebadadeli and Boule-Boule, all of them concerned with the inadvertent breaking of an egg. Anyone who has ever had to clean up a broken raw egg has confronted the viscous, slippery and wildly elusive egg white. It slips, slides and flows in every direction, causing frustration in adults and revulsion and disgust in children.

Although raw egg whites are about as "yucky" a substance as we are likely to encounter in the kitchen, they are one of the great miracles of the science and art of cookery. Previous volumes have dealt in great detail with the magical role of egg whites in soufflés and spongecakes, but equally astonishing is the ability of the egg white to be transformed into a delectable, crunchy meringue.

Several sources credit a Swiss pastry chef by the name of Gasparini with inventing (or, more probably, perfecting) the meringue in 1720, and since Gasparini lived in a town called Mehrinyghen, his creation was named after it. In short order, the royalty of Europe took up meringues with great enthusiasm. When it became fashionable for kings and queens to dabble in the culinary arts, Marie Antoinette, who enjoyed playing house in a specially built "cottage" at Versailles, is said to have made meringues with her own hands. It is even rumored that she perfected the *vacherin*, a decorative meringue bowl that served as an edible container for a variety of sweet creams and exotic fruits and berries.

"To the American cook," wrote the great chef Henri Paul Pellaprat, "the word meringue generally means the topping for a pie, which is soft meringue. However, to the French cook, it more often means hard meringue [such as Marie Antoinette's vacherin], used as a base or bowl for a dessert." (*The Great Book of French Cuisine*) A quick perusal of any of the classical texts on French cookery will yield up the following list of dramatic and luscious gâteaux and desserts based on meringue: *le succès, la dacquoise, le progrès marjolaine, gâteaux japonais,* and *gâteaux à la Bennich,* among many others. What all of these have in common is that they are layer-cake extravaganzas made with layers of hard meringue instead of flour-based cake.

Meringues appear in many other guises, shapes and forms. Sometimes they float in a sea of creamy custard as in *oeufs à la neige* (eggs in snow) or a similar dessert called *île flottante* (floating island), sometimes they are shaped with a pastry bag into beguiling and artistic shapes, such as tiny white kisses or the woodland mushrooms that are used to decorate a *bûche de Noël.* Even the broken bits of a hard meringue are sometimes put to use in a classic French dessert called a *caprice,* in which the broken meringue is folded into a liqueur-flavored whipped cream.

Although the meringue was invented in France, and all the meringue creations we've discussed thus far are French in origin, some of the most famous meringue desserts are from other countries. One of the best-known of these is the Pavlova, created in Australia for the Russian ballerina Anna Pavlova, who was on tour there in the 1930s. The anonymous chef anticipated the recent popularizing of kiwi fruit in nouvelle cuisine when he featured it in the Pavlova, which, according to Waverley Root, was named after the ballerina because "it is as light on the stomach as Pavlova was light on her feet."(*Food*) In addition, there is, of course, our own baked Alaska (originally called Alaska-Florida), the ice-cream and hot meringue dessert said by some to have to have resulted from experiments with the properties of egg whites performed by Benjamin Thompson, an American physicist working in England. Culinary writer Baron Brisse wrote enthusiastically about the baked Alaska, claiming that it gives a gourmet "the double pleasure of biting through piping hot crust and cooling the palate on contact with fragrant ices." (*Larousse Gastronomique*)

Whatever its shape, the wondrous meringue imparts a sense of fantasy to a stunning array of dessert dishes and can easily transform an ordinary sweet into a lavish and extraordinary dessert.

MERINGUE

When air is beaten into egg whites, their volume is dramatically increased. If sugar is then added, a meringue is made, which can be cooked briefly to remain soft inside, or at length in a slow oven to make crisp shells.

There are four kinds of meringues discussed here: Standard Meringue, also called Hard Meringue, can be used for any preparation needing meringue, but it is particularly good for making small or large shells, small meringues for decoration, and pie topping.

Cooked Meringue can be used for the same purposes, but it is particularly good for piping out nests, rings, layers, etc., as the basis for more elaborate desserts. It is also a good choice for meringue baskets since it holds its shape somewhat better than Standard Meringue when made into large containers.

American Meringue has a soft center when baked. It is the best choice for making cake layers and vacherins, and a dessert such as a Pavlova. This meringue is not piped but is piled onto the pan or baking sheet.

Italian Meringue is also used to top desserts, but in this case the desserts are all very light to begin with—delicate cakes, pies, and custards. It is also folded into other ingredients to make fruit-flavored frozen soufflés and some mousses.

To make meringue successfully, the ingredients must be in the correct proportions.

Ingredients

Egg Whites. These are the basis of meringues. Use large eggs for the greatest amount of egg white. It is better if the eggs are a few days old, as the white will then have thickened somewhat and will be easier to whisk than the thinner white of very fresh eggs; however, unless you buy your eggs fresh from the farm, you need not worry about this short "aging"; by the time the egg gets to the store, it will have aged sufficiently. Once the egg is a few days old, the fresher it is, the greater the amount of foam when beaten and the better the flavor.

It is easier to separate eggs when they are cold, and there is less chance of breaking the yolk. But after separating, let the egg whites reach room temperature, for they will give greater volume than when cold, and will whip more easily.

Stabilizer. To stabilize egg whites and make them hold their shape when whipped, cream of tartar and sometimes salt are added. A pinch of either for each egg is enough; it should be added to the whites when they start to foam.

Sugar. Sugar is added to egg whites to give flavor and body and to make it possible to cook them without having them collapse. Superfine sugar is preferred because it dissolves more quickly. Granulated sugar is coarser and can produce a "weepy" meringue with little bubbles of caramel on the surface. However, in a pinch you can use granulated sugar; the important thing is to be sure the sugar is completely dissolved in the beaten egg whites. If you take a pinch of the meringue between thumb and forefinger and rub the fingers together, there should be no grainy feeling. From 1 to 4 tablespoons sugar is used for each egg white. If too little sugar is used, the meringue may collapse, and the sweetness expected in a meringue will be missing. If too much is used, the meringue will be "weepy." Confectioners' sugar is used in Cooked Meringues.

Cornstarch. This is added to American Meringue to keep it from becoming too sticky.

Equipment

Very little equipment is needed for making meringues.

A *large bowl* in which to whisk egg whites is the most important item. The classic bowl is an unlined copper bowl. A chemical reaction takes place when the moist egg whites come in contact with the copper; this stabilizes the egg whites as they mount. However, these bowls are mainly found in professional kitchens. For the ordinary home kitchen, a stainless-steel bowl is best. Glass or pottery bowls can also be used but the whites may not climb as well in them and therefore won't mount as high. Do not use plastic or aluminum. It is impossible to keep plastic perfectly fat-free because it tends to absorb minute amounts of foods mixed or stored in it; aluminum tends to give the whites a gray tinge. For a meringue the bowl must be scrupulously clean, with no trace of fat, since fat prevents the proper development of the foam. One good trick is to wipe the entire inside of the bowl with a paper towel dipped in vinegar or lemon juice. The acid also helps to stabilize the meringue.

A *balloon whisk* is the best tool to use for beating egg whites; it allows the maximum amount of air to be beaten into them, giving the greatest volume and lightest texture. The whisk, like the bowl, must be clean and dry. It too can be wiped with a paper towel dipped in vinegar or lemon juice. Dry thoroughly. An electric beater speeds the job but gives a denser texture and less volume than hand-beating with the whisk. The speed of the power-driven tool can break down the air bubbles, and can result in overbeating, which causes the foam to collapse. Rotary beaters are better than electric beaters, but not as good as a whisk.

Baking sheets and loose-bottomed cake pans are essential.

A *pastry bag* with assorted tips is useful for many meringues and essential for some.

Making Standard Meringue

Separate the eggs (see Volume 9 Index). If any trace of yolk gets into the white, it will interfere with the whisking, since egg yolk contains fat and even a speck of fat can prevent the whites from mounting. If you should accidentally get a speck of yolk in the bowl, fish it out with the edge of a piece of eggshell or with a spoon. Let the whites come to room temperature or set them over a bowl of warm water to heat them briefly.

Whisk until whites foam, then add cream of tartar and salt as specified in the recipe. Whisk slowly at first, tilting the bowl to encourage maximum incorporation of air. The whites will first turn foamy and then begin to thicken. At this point increase the whisking speed. The whites will soon turn thick and close in texture. And if the whisk is lifted from the mixture, the whites that cling to it form soft mounds with floppy tops that fall back into themselves.

It is now time to add the superfine sugar. Sprinkle it, 1 tablespoon at a time, and whisk until it is dissolved before adding more. Continue until half the sugar has been added and dissolved. At this stage the mixture will form a thick foam that looks glossy. The sugar is whisked in gradually because the meringue would collapse if too much were added at once. Using a metal spoon or a rubber spatula for folding, add the remaining sugar, folding in half at a time. Continue folding until the sugar has been evenly distributed throughout the meringue and the sugar is dissolved. The meringue should not be grainy. When you are done, you should be able to turn the bowl upside down without the meringue falling out. When the whisk is withdrawn from the batter, the meringue that is lifted by the whisk should stand in stiff peaks with tops that curl slightly but don't fold over onto themselves.

As soon as this stage has been reached, the meringue should be used or it will gradually begin to separate and collapse.

Cooked Meringue

This kind of meringue is said to be cooked because it is beaten over warm water. The ingredients for cooked meringue are similar to those for standard meringue—egg whites and sugar—but the sugar used is confectioners' rather than superfine. Usually ½ cup confectioners' sugar is used for each egg white. Be sure to sift the sugar before using it, as it can be lumpy. When this mixture is whisked over heat, it makes a firm, glossy meringue, ideal for piping and baskets.

Traditionally cooked meringue is flavored with vanilla. Use 1 teaspoon vanilla extract to flavor a meringue made with 4 or 5 egg whites.

Making Cooked Meringue

First sift the confectioners' sugar. Select a large bowl for whisking the meringue and a saucepan in which you can nest the bowl so it is suspended. Fill the bottom of the saucepan with tepid water.

Separate the eggs according to the instructions given under Standard Meringue. Whisk until foamy. Add ⅛ teaspoon each cream of tartar and salt for 4 egg whites. Then start to whisk in the confectioners' sugar, 1 teaspoon at a time. Whisking in such a small amount at a time insures that each spoonful is dissolved. Set the pan containing the tepid water over low heat and place the bowl of egg whites over the water, making sure the water does not touch the bottom of the bowl.

Standard Meringue

4	large egg whites
⅛	teaspoon cream of tartar
⅛	teaspoon salt
1	cup superfine sugar

4 As the whites begin to turn foamy, add cream of tartar and salt. Increase beating speed until the mixture is thick and white.

Cooked Meringue

2	cups confectioners' sugar
4	egg whites
⅛	teaspoon cream of tartar
⅛	teaspoon salt
1	teaspoon vanilla extract

1 Sift the sugar. Select a pan into which you can nest a large bowl for egg whites. Add tepid water to the pan.

1 Drop the egg whites into a grease-free and moisture-free large bowl. Let come to room temperature.

2 Break the egg whites up with a fork.

3 Tilt the bowl away from you and start whisking the egg whites.

5 To test if whites are ready, lift up the whisk. The mixture should be thick and close in texture.

6 Add ½ cup of the sugar, 1 tablespoon at a time, and whisk after each addition until the sugar is dissolved.

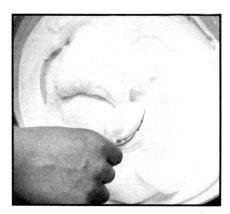

7 Fold in half of remaining sugar with a metal spoon or rubber spatula. Fold in the rest the same way.

2 Place egg whites in bowl and whisk until foamy. Add cream of tartar and salt and whisk until thick.

3 Whisk in the sugar, 1 teaspoon at a time. Whisk in the vanilla. Set pan over low heat and place bowl over the water. Water must not touch bottom of bowl.

4 Whisk the mixture over low heat until it thickens, 10 to 15 minutes by hand. When meringue is ready, the whisk will leave a thick trail.

Meringue Cake with American Meringue

Use this cake as a base, filling the hollow or spreading the layers with whipped cream and/or poached fruit or fruit purées flavored with liqueurs, if desired.

4	egg whites
⅛	teaspoon cream of tartar
⅛	teaspoon salt
1⅛	cups superfine sugar
1	teaspoon vanilla extract
1	teaspoon lemon juice or vinegar
4	teaspoons cornstarch
4	ounces ground blanched almonds

1 Butter an 8-inch loose-bottomed cake pan and dust with flour; or line the base with cooking parchment.

2 Preheat oven to 375°F. Bring egg whites to room temperature. Whisk until foamy. Add cream of tartar and salt and whisk until thick and close in texture.

3 Beat in sugar, 1 teaspoon at a time. Test to see that sugar is dissolved by rubbing mixture against side of bowl with a knife.

4 Whisk in vanilla, lemon juice or vinegar and cornstarch. Stop whisking as soon as amalgamated, about 2 minutes.

5 With metal spoon or rubber spatula fold in ground almonds with a figure-eight movement. Stop folding as soon as amalgamated.

6 Pile the meringue in the prepared pan; level the top slightly and make a shallow indentation in the center. Bake for 40 minutes.

OR To make a layer cake, divide the meringue between 2 pans. Bake in the center of the oven for 40 minutes.

7 Cool slightly, allowing the meringue to shrink away from pan, then push up loose bottom. Gently peel paper from meringue. Cool.

Making a Large Meringue Basket

To make this basket, you will need a double recipe of Cooked Meringue. Do not prepare both at once. The first batch is used to make the basket base and sides; the second is used to decorate. Make the first batch before step 1 and the second before step 6. Cooked Meringue will keep its shape longer than Standard Meringue, but it is always better to use the meringue as soon as it is ready.

1 Cover two baking sheets with cooking parchment or oiled wax paper. Draw two equal 6- to 8-inch circles on each piece of paper.

2 Fit a pastry bag with a ½-inch éclair tip and fill it with the meringue. Pipe a circle, following one of the pencil lines. Fill in the circle with more meringue.

3 Pipe meringue around the outside of remaining 3 circles, covering the pencil lines and leaving the center empty.

4 Bake in a 225°F oven for 50 to 60 minutes, until meringue is dry and crisp.

5 Gently peel paper from hollow circles. Place the circles on the solid base. Make the second batch of meringue.

6 Fit a pastry bag with a ½-inch star tip. Fill with meringue and carefully pipe vertical lines around the basket.

7 Pipe a decorative border around the base and top of the basket to cover the ends of the piped lines.

8 Return meringue to the oven and bake for 60 minutes longer. When baked, remove from oven and peel off the paper.

Meringue Pie Topping

1 Spread meringue over prepared pie. Make sure meringue touches edges of pastry or pie dish. Shape top with spoon handle or icing spatula.

OR Pipe on prepared meringue through a pastry bag fitted with a piping tube. Make rings, starting with the outside ring.

2 If desired, scatter superfine sugar over the meringue for a sweeter topping, or use slivered almonds for a textured topping.

Meringue Shells

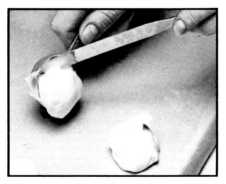 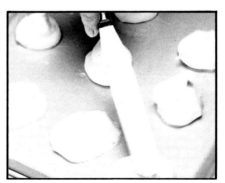 

1 Spoon 1 to 2 tablespoons of meringue batter on prepared baking sheet (see Introduction). Use more for larger shells. Round each shape with wet knife.

2 Bake meringues in a preheated 225°F oven for 1 ½ to 2 hours for small shells or 2 to 2½ hours for large, or until shells are crisp and dry.

3 Sandwich meringue shells in pairs with fruit, cream or ice cream, alone or mixed together.

Meringue Nests

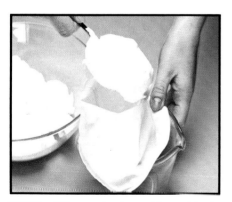 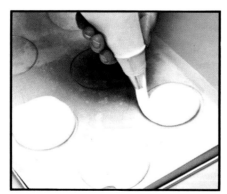 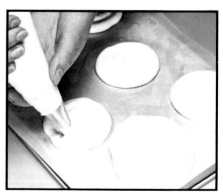

1 Fit a pastry bag with a ½-inch star or éclair tip. Fill the bag with cooked meringue.

2 On a prepared baking sheet (see Introduction), pipe a round 4 inches in diameter.

3 Using the ½-inch star tip, pipe a ring around the outer edge of the solid round. Pipe another ring on top of the first.

Meringue Stars

3 Bake at 425°F for 5 to 7 minutes, or until the top of the meringue is streaked with gold.

4 To decorate, dip a skewer into melted chocolate and dribble patterns or lines of chocolate across each meringue.

4 Bake in preheated 225°F oven for 1 to 2 hours, till crisp and dry. Cool completely. Fill with fresh fruit and cream or ice cream.

Whisk the meringue until it is thick. When the meringue is ready, a thick trail will be left on it when the whisk is lifted. It usually takes 10 to 15 minutes of beating to reach this stage with a hand-held whisk, or 8 minutes with an electric beater. (Although an electric beater is not recommended for standard meringue, it is all right to use one for cooked meringue.)

As soon as the whisk leaves a trail in the meringue, remove the bowl from the heat.

American Meringue for Vacherin and Cake Layers

American meringue is a thick mixture slightly different from Standard Meringue and Cooked Meringue. Egg whites and sugar are used in the same way and in the same proportion as for Cooked Meringue. However, superfine sugar replaces the confectioners' sugar because it helps to give a marshmallow texture to the center.

Cornstarch is used as an ingredient in the meringue to help dry it out during baking and prevent "weeping" of the sugar, which would make the cake too sticky. Usually 1 teaspoon cornstarch is used for each egg white, although this may vary. In some recipes containing ground nuts, which help absorb the sugar, cornstarch may be omitted.

A little lemon juice or vinegar is also added to help produce the soft center of a meringue cake. The juice or vinegar has no effect on the flavor of the meringue, but it changes the structure of the sugar, making the cake soft in the center and crisp on the outside. In some recipes you may find a mixture of vinegar and lemon juice being used, which makes the meringue very white. Usually ½ teaspoon lemon juice or vinegar is used for every 2 egg whites. More acid may be used in a Pavlova, as it should be very soft in the center. If you are using vinegar, it can be cider vinegar, white vinegar or malt vinegar.

Vanilla extract is the usual flavoring for meringue cakes. Coffee Essence (see Volume 1 Index) may be used in the same way. In nut-flavored

1 Using a pastry bag fitted with a star tip, pipe rosettes of meringue batter onto prepared baking sheets (see Introduction).

2 Bake in a preheated 225°F oven for 1½ to 2 hours, or until stars are crisp and dry. Use to decorate fresh fruit or fruit compote.

3 Alternatively, sandwich meringue stars with cream or fruit and cream. Or use to top custards or decorate cakes.

5 Alternatively, spread a baked meringue base with whipped cream and edge with a crown of meringue stars.

6 Fill the center of the crown with fruit and whipped cream and decorate with more whipped cream.

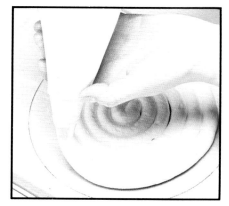

7 To make a tiered meringue cake, fit a piping bag with a large plain tip. Pipe a large round.

1 Using a medium-size rope tip on a pastry bag, pipe a round spiral of meringue batter on a prepared baking sheet.

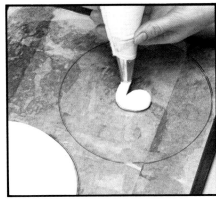

2 Pipe 2 other rounds in the same way. Bake in a 275°F oven for 1 hour, or until crisp outside, but soft inside.

3 Remove 1 meringue layer and place on a serving plate. Spread with fruit and whipped cream or other filling.

4 Place another meringue layer on top of the filling. Cover with more filling and top with the final meringue layer.

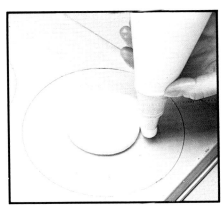

8 Pipe another round 1 inch smaller than the first and a final round 1 inch smaller than the second.

9 Bake and cool layers. With the largest round on the bottom, sandwich tiers together with whipped cream and fruit.

meringue cakes, ground almonds or hazelnuts are folded into the meringue batter before baking. The amount used varies from recipe to recipe. It is unwise to experiment with the amount of flavoring for meringue as the balance of the ingredients might be altered, causing the meringue to fail.

Making American Meringue

Separate the eggs (see Volume 9 Index). Beat egg whites until foamy, add salt and cream of tartar, then whisk until the whites are stiff. Beating to the stiff stage is essential for this type of meringue or it will collapse when the sugar is added. Whisk the cream of tartar and salt into the egg whites. Then whisk in the sugar, 1 teaspoon at a time, making sure each addition is dissolved and has been evenly distributed before you add the next. Rub a little of the batter between your thumb and forefinger; if the batter feels granular, the sugar is not dissolved. Undissolved sugar is a particular danger when making American meringue, as it can produce a "weepy" meringue that will stick stubbornly to the baking sheet or the lining paper. It can also break down the aeration and the mixture will then collapse. Adding and properly incorporating the sugar will take about 8 minutes.

Add the lemon juice or vinegar, cornstarch and flavoring all at once and quickly whisk them in. These ingredients are added together rather than separately to cut down the whisking time and lessen the possibility of breaking down the air bubbles.

If the meringue is to have a nutty flavor, the nuts must be ground very fine and folded in after the cornstarch and acid. Fold the nuts in gently with a figure-eight movement, using a metal spoon or rubber spatula.

Italian Meringue

This meringue has the sugar added in the form of a cooked sugar syrup. It is much like Buttercream with Sugar Syrup (see Volume 5 Index), but of course lacks butter and egg yolks. It is used to top very light-textured cakes,

Chocolate Meringue Pudding

6 portions

The base	The chocolate sauce	The meringue topping

The base

⅔	cup all-purpose flour
2	teaspoons baking powder
½	cup powdered cocoa
¼	cup superfine sugar
2	egg yolks
4	tablespoons milk

The chocolate sauce

1½	tablespoons butter
6	ounces sweet chocolate

The meringue topping

2	large egg whites
⅓	cup superfine sugar
1	tablespoon granulated sugar

1 Preheat the oven to 400°F. Butter a 2-cup ovenproof dish. Sift flour and cocoa together. Cream butter and sugar and add flour-cocoa mixture.

2 Combine the egg yolks and milk and add, beating into mixture until incorporated.

3 With a spatula, scrape the mixture into the prepared dish and bake in the oven for 20 minutes.

4 Put sauce ingredients in a bowl. Melt over, but not in, hot, but not boiling, water and stir until smooth and shiny.

5 Remove base from the oven. Increase oven temperature to 425°F. Spread the sauce over the base.

6 Beat egg whites until meringue is glossy and stiff peaks form.

7 Fold in superfine sugar with light movements, being careful not to deflate the whites as you fold.

8 Pile the meringue on top of the pudding, making sure to spread it out to the edges of the dish.

9 Return pudding to the oven and bake for 3 to 5 minutes, or until the meringue is streaked with gold. Serve immediately.

84

Pavlova

In Australia this cake, named for the famous ballerina Anna Pavlova, is topped with passion fruit, kiwis, mangoes and papaws. We have substituted more readily available fruit, but by all means use tropical fruits if you can find them. The cake is usually baked on a baking sheet or in a springform pan.

6 portions

4	egg whites	1	cup superfine sugar	4	teaspoons cornstarch
1/8	teaspoon cream of tartar	2	teaspoons lemon juice or vinegar	1	teaspoon vanilla extract
1/8	teaspoon salt				

Filling

1 1/4	cups heavy cream, whipped	2	peaches, peeled, pitted and quartered	4	ounces grapes, peeled and seeded
2	bananas				

1 Line a baking sheet with oiled wax paper. Set oven to 275°F.

2 Whisk egg whites until foamy. Add cream of tartar and salt and whisk until egg whites are thick and close in texture.

3 Whisk sugar into whites, about 1 teaspoon at a time, making sure sugar is dissolved before adding more.

4 Whisk lemon juice or vinegar, cornstarch and vanilla into the meringue. Stop whisking as soon as amalgamated.

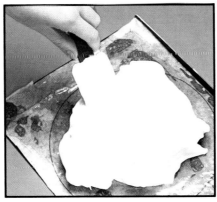

5 Pile the meringue on the prepared baking sheet. With a spatula make a slight hollow in the center.

6 Bake on the bottom of the oven for 1 to 1¼ hours, or until meringue is lightly colored on the outside.

7 When baked, carefully peel off the paper. Cool the meringue on a wire rack.

8 Spoon whipped cream into the center of the meringue.

9 Peel and slice bananas and arrange around the edge. Pile the peach quarters in the center and top with the grapes.

pies or puddings. It is also used when making certain fruit-flavored frozen soufflés. Like other meringues, it can be piped or spooned out to make shells or nests. It is used like buttercream to fill cakes and is a good choice for desserts such as baked Alaska.

Although Italian meringue is soft and smooth it does not deflate quickly. For this meringue you will need an electric mixer, for you will have to keep beating the egg whites while pouring in the sugar syrup very slowly and carefully.

Making Italian Meringue

Dissolve the sugar in half its volume of water, stirring constantly over low heat; there should not be a single grain of undissolved sugar in the solution, for it might burn when the heat is increased. Increase heat to moderate and bring the syrup to a boil, boiling until the syrup reaches the firm ball stage (242° to 248°F on a candy thermometer). Meanwhile, beat the egg whites with cream of tartar and salt until stiff. Still beating the whites, pour the hot syrup into them in a slow steady stream and continue until all the syrup is incorporated and the meringue is stiff and glossy, about 10 minutes with an electric beater. Now set the bowl of meringue in a larger container of ice water and add flavoring extract, if you are using any. Fold it in, and continue to fold the meringue over and over for about 3 minutes. Let the meringue stand in the ice water for 10 minutes, folding it over now and then. The meringue is now ready to use.

Baking Meringues

When baking meringues, the oven must be preheated to the temperature specified; allow 15 minutes for preheating. The way meringue is baked depends on how it is to be used.

If meringue is to be used as a topping, pile it on the base, spreading it edge to edge with a spatula. It must touch the pastry edge or the edge of the pudding or custard dish all around, for meringue tends to shrink during baking and will pull away if not an-chored, thus ruining the appearance of the dish. Use the handle of a spoon or an icing spatula to make the meringue stand in peaks and swirls. Alternatively, put the meringue in a pastry bag fitted with a star or rope tip and pipe the meringue on the dessert base. If you want a soft meringue, brown on the outside but of a marshmallow consistency inside, bake at 425°F for 5 to 7 minutes. For a crisper topping, bake at 350°F for 30 minutes.

Meringue shells and bases for cakes and baskets are dried in a very low oven rather than baked. The aim is to make the meringue dry and crisp while keeping it from coloring.

There are several ways to prepare a baking pan or sheet for these dry meringues. The pan can be oiled or buttered and sprinkled with flour or cornstarch (be sure to shake out any excess).

Another and easier method to prepare a baking pan or sheet is to line it with plain brown or white paper, which will prevent overbrowning of the bottom of the meringues. Other choices are aluminum foil, wax paper, cooking parchment and baking pan lining paper, especially designed for such uses. Sometimes the recipe will say that the pan lining should be brushed with oil; use a tasteless and odorless vegetable oil.

If you are piping out circles or rounds on a floured pan, mark the circle on the flour or cornstarch coating; place a pan or cookie cutter of the right size on the coating and run a knife tip around it to mark the size and shape.

If you are going to be piping out carefully shaped meringues on a paper-lined baking sheet, choose transparent baking paper. With a pencil make the design needed, then turn the paper over so that no pencil lead can be absorbed by the meringue. Stick the paper to the baking sheet with a tiny dab of the meringue so it does not slide around when you are piping.

If a pan is called for, be sure it has a removable bottom as it is almost impossible to get a meringue out of a pan with a fixed base. Prepare the bottom in the same way as you would the baking sheet, with either oil and flour or cornstarch or with a paper lining.

Preheat the oven to 225°F and place the meringues on the lowest shelf. Bake the shells or layers for 2 to 3 hours, and, if necessary, leave the oven door slightly ajar to keep the meringues from browning.

Another way to bake dry meringues is to heat the oven to 400°F, put the meringues on the oven floor, and turn off the oven. Do not open the door for at least 5 hours.

There are other ways to bake meringues, but unless you are inventing your own dessert, it is best to follow the directions given in the recipes.

Serving Ideas for Meringues

Aside from the familiar pie toppings and the small shells sandwiched with whipped cream, more elaborate desserts can be made using meringue layers like cake layers, or meringue and cake layers together. For spectacular results, make baskets or vacherins. While the term "vacherin" is sometimes used for cakes made of meringue layers, it is more accurately a meringue container, sometimes baked on a base of sweet tart pastry, filled with ice cream or whipped cream, crème Chantilly, buttercream or pastry cream, topped with or mixed with fruits, especially soft fruits such as strawberries.

Do not fill shells, nests, baskets or layers until just before serving as the filling will soak into the meringue and soften it if it has to wait.

For fillings use ice cream, scooped into balls, plain or flavored with liqueur, or mixed with fruits or fruit purée. Whipped cream mixed with fruit purée is also good; melted chocolate and liqueurs are good with cream.

Meringue topping is good on small tarts as well as pies, on baked apples or pears, stewed fruits and custards.

Meringues baked until completely dry and crisp can be crumbled and mixed into ice cream that has been softened for mixing and is then refrozen. Meringue crumbs also give texture to custards and make delicious crumb toppings on many desserts.

Fruit Nests

8 portions

1	recipe Cooked Meringue	6	ounces fresh strawberries
1	cup heavy cream	4	tablespoons red-currant
2	tablespoons kirsch		jelly
4	peaches		

Preheat oven to 225°F. Line two baking sheets with cooking parchment or oiled aluminum foil. Fit a pastry bag with a ½-inch éclair tip. Gently spoon the meringue into the bag. Making a spiral, pipe a solid circle 4 inches in diameter. Pipe 7 more circles in the same fashion, being careful to leave space between them. Now fit the piping bag with a ½-inch star tip. Pipe around the edges of the solid circles to make sides. Bake the nests on the bottom shelf of the oven for about 2 hours, or until they are dry and crisp and lightly colored. Gently peel away the paper on the bottom and cool the meringues on a wire rack.

Whip the cream until stiff. Stir the kirsch into the cream and spread some of the mixture in the base of each meringue nest, reserving any leftover cream. Bring a saucepan of water to a boil and, off the heat, blanch the peaches by submerging them in the water for 1 minute. Peel the peaches; halve and pit them, and cut each peach into 8 slices. Place 4 peach slices in each meringue nest, arranging the slices around the edges so there is a space in the middle. Wash, pat dry, hull, and halve the strawberries. Divide the berries among the nests, filling the centers. Place the red-currant jelly in a heavy pan set over low heat. When melted, brush over the fruits to glaze them. Serve the fruit nests as soon as they are ready. If there is cream left over, use it to decorate the tops.

Igloo Pudding

6 portions

2	egg whites	3	whole eggs
	pinch of cream of tartar	¼	teaspoon vanilla extract
	pinch of salt	6	tablespoons brandy
⅞	cup superfine sugar	1	cup heavy cream

Set the 2 egg whites aside to come to room temperature. Preheat oven to 225°F. Line a baking sheet with cooking parchment paper or oiled aluminum foil. When the whites have warmed, beat them with a whisk or rotary beater until they are foamy. Add cream of tartar and salt and beat until they are thick and close in texture. Add 1 tablespoon of the sugar and continue beating for 1 minute. With a metal spoon or rubber spatula, carefully fold in 7 tablespoons more sugar. The meringue should be stiff and glossy. Drop tablespoons of the meringue on the lined baking sheet. Bake the meringues in the oven for 2 to 2½ hours, or until they are pale golden brown and crisp throughout. If meringues begin to brown too much or too soon, open the oven door. Remove baking sheet from the oven and set meringues aside to cool.

About 20 minutes before meringues are done, separate remaining 3 eggs. When meringues are removed from oven, beat the yolks, vanilla and brandy together with a fork until well blended. In another bowl, beat the cream with a whisk or rotary beater until stiff. In a third bowl beat the 3 egg whites with a whisk or rotary beater until thick and close in texture. Add 1 tablespoon of the remaining sugar and continue beating for 1 minute. With a metal spoon or rubber spatula, carefully fold in the rest of the sugar. Pour the egg-yolk mixture onto the whipped cream and fold the two mixtures together. Gently fold the beaten egg whites into the cream mixture. Spoon the pudding mixture into a lightly oiled 2-quart freezer dish. Cover the dish and freeze for 1 hour.

When the meringues are cool, crumble them into a large mixing bowl. Remove pudding from the freezer and fold in the crumbled meringues. Return the dish to the freezer for another hour, or until the pudding is hard.

At serving time, dip the dish quickly into hot water. Place a serving plate upside down over the pudding. Holding the dish and plate firmly together, turn them over. Give the dish a vigorous shake. The pudding should slide out easily. Serve at once.

Hazelnut Meringue Cake with Raspberries

6 portions

4	egg whites	1	teaspoon vanilla extract
4	ounces shelled hazelnuts	1	cup heavy cream
⅛	teaspoon cream of tartar	2	pints fresh raspberries, or
⅛	teaspoon salt		15 ounces unsweetened
1⅛	cups superfine sugar		frozen raspberries
1	teaspoon lemon juice or	4	tablespoons confectioners'
	vinegar		sugar

Drop the egg whites into a large mixing bowl and let come to room temperature. Grind the hazelnuts in a nut grinder or food processor until fine. Line two 8-inch loose-bottomed cake pans or two baking sheets with cooking parchment or oiled foil. Preheat oven to 275°F. Whisk the egg whites, add cream of tartar and salt, and whisk until they are thick and close in texture. Whisk in the superfine sugar, 1 teaspoon at a time, making sure each addition is dissolved before adding the next. Beat until the meringue is stiff. Whisk in the lemon juice or vinegar and the vanilla. Fold in the ground hazelnuts. Divide the mixture equally between the cake pans or spread into two 8-inch rounds on the baking sheets. Bake for 1 hour, or until lightly colored and set. When the meringues are ready, carefully peel off the paper and cool the layers.

Whip the cream until stiff. Wash and hull the fresh raspberries. Spread a thick layer of the whipped cream over one of the meringue layers, reserving the rest of the cream. Top the cream with half of the raspberries. Place the second meringue layer on top. Decorate the cake with remaining whipped cream and 8 to 12 whole raspberries.

Make a Melba sauce: Sift the confectioners' sugar into a bowl. Purée the remaining raspberries and mix with the sugar. Serve the cake with the Melba sauce.

Italian Meringue

1	cup granulated sugar		pinch of cream of tartar
½	cup water		pinch of salt
3	egg whites	½	teaspoon flavoring extract

Combine the sugar and the water in a heavy saucepan set over low heat. Stir constantly with a wooden spoon until the sugar has completely dissolved. Increase heat to moderate and bring the syrup to a boil, boiling it until it reaches 242° to 248°F on a candy thermometer, or until a small amount of syrup dropped into cold water forms a firm ball.

Meanwhile, beat the egg whites with a whisk or rotary beater until foamy. Add the cream of tartar and salt and continue beating till the whites form stiff peaks. Remove the syrup pan from the heat. Switch to an electric mixer, and while continuing to beat the egg whites, pour the syrup into them in a slow, steady stream. Continue beating for about 10 minutes, or until all the syrup is incorporated and the meringue is stiff and glossy.

Set the bowl of meringue in a larger container of ice water and fold in the flavoring with a rubber spatula. Fold the meringue over and over for 3 minutes, then let it stand for 10 minutes, folding it occasionally. It is now ready to use.

Meringue Martinique

8 portions

1 recipe Standard Meringue	4 ounces semisweet chocolate
1¼ cups heavy cream	1 tablespoon unsalted butter
3 tablespoons rum	

Preheat oven to 250°F. Line two large baking sheets with cooking parchment or oiled aluminum foil. Fit a pastry bag with a plain tip and fill with the meringue. Pipe 16 meringue shells on the baking sheets. Alternatively, use two large spoons to shape the meringue shells. Bake the shells in the center of the oven for 1½ hours, or until they are crisp on the outside and slightly sticky on the inside, and pale beige in color. If meringues begin to brown too much or too soon, open the oven door. Halfway through the baking time, reverse the baking sheets so that the one that was on the bottom is on the top.

Remove baking sheets from the oven. With a spatula, turn the meringues over. With a fingertip, gently press the underside of each meringue to make a small hollow. Return baking sheets to the oven and bake for 30 minutes longer.

Cool the meringues for 5 minutes. Using the spatula, carefully transfer meringues to a wire rack to cool completely.

Beat the cream in a bowl with a whisk or rotary beater until thick. Add 2 tablespoons of the rum and continue beating until the cream is stiff. Cover the bowl and put it in the refrigerator to chill for at least 1 hour. Just before serving, sandwich the meringue shells together with the cream and arrange meringues on a serving plate.

Break the chocolate into small pieces. Cut butter into tiny bits. Melt the chocolate with remaining rum in a small saucepan over low heat, stirring occasionally. As soon as the chocolate is melted, remove pan from heat. Beat in the butter, a piece at a time. When all the butter has been absorbed, trickle a little of the chocolate sauce over each meringue. Serve immediately.

Lemon Meringue Pie

4 portions

2 eggs	1¼ cups water
1 recipe Short-Crust Pastry (see Volume 2 Index)	2 tablespoons cornstarch
1 large lemon	1 tablespoon unsalted butter
2 tablespoons granulated sugar	pinch of cream of tartar
	pinch of salt
	½ cup superfine sugar

Separate the eggs, cover lightly and set aside. Preheat oven to 400°F. Roll out the pastry and use it to line a 7-inch flan ring or pie pan. (If there is excess pastry, wrap in plastic wrap and refrigerate for another use.) Bake the pastry blind (see Volume 2, page 86) in the center of the oven for 10 minutes. Remove weights and lining and bake for 5 minutes longer. Remove the baked pie shell from the oven and let it cool.

Peel the rind from the lemon with a swivel peeler and squeeze the juice. Put lemon rind, granulated sugar and the water in a saucepan. Set over low heat and stir until the sugar is dissolved. Bring to a boil and boil for 1 minute. Remove pan from heat. In a large bowl blend the cornstarch with the lemon juice until smooth. Pour the sugar syrup through a fine sieve onto the cornstarch paste, stirring all the time. Add the reserved egg yolks and the butter to the syrup mixture and beat until the butter has melted and the mixture has become thick. If it does not seem thick enough, return it all to the saucepan and heat gently, stirring constantly, until it is thick.

Reduce oven heat to 300°F. Remove the cooked pie shell from the flan ring if you have used it; if you have used a pie pan, leave the shell in the pan. Spoon the lemon custard into the pastry. Whisk the egg whites until foamy, add the cream of tartar and salt, and whisk until thick and close in texture. Whisk in half of the superfine sugar, 1 tablespoon at a time, then fold in the rest in two batches, reserving 1 teaspoon of the sugar. Pile the meringue on top of the lemon filling. Spread from the edge to the center, making sure the meringue reaches the pastry edge all around. Make swirls and peaks in the meringue with the handle of a spoon. Alternatively, pipe meringue onto the filling with a large star or rope tip. Sprinkle remaining sugar over the meringue and bake in the center of the oven for 20 to 30 minutes, or until meringue is crisp and golden. Serve warm.

Variation: For lime meringue pie, substitute 2 large or 3 small limes for the lemon.

Chocolate Chinchilla

6 portions

6	egg whites	¼	teaspoon cream of tartar
6	tablespoons sweetened	¼	teaspoon salt
	powdered cocoa	1	cup superfine sugar
1	teaspoon ground cinnamon		

Preheat oven to 350°F. Bring the egg whites to room temperature. Butter a 5-cup ovenproof dish. Sift the powdered cocoa and cinnamon together in a bowl. Turn the egg whites into a large bowl, whisk until foamy, add cream of tartar and salt, and whisk until egg whites are thick and close in texture. Whisk in ½ cup of the sugar, 1 tablespoon at a time. Fold in the remainder, half at a time. Add the mixed chocolate and cinnamon, folding it in with a metal spoon until evenly distributed.

Pile the meringue into the buttered dish and bake in the center of the oven for 45 minutes, or until golden. Leave in a draft-free place to cool. Serve with Custard Sauce (see Volume 11 Index), omitting the ginger and flavoring the sauce with 1 to 2 tablespoons rum, or with light cream.

Queen Anne's Custard

6 to 8 portions

2½	cups milk
1	1-inch piece of vanilla bean
2	whole eggs
2	egg yolks
¼	cup superfine sugar

¼	cup orange-flavored liqueur (for example, Grand Marnier, Cointreau, or Triple Sec)
1	recipe Italian Meringue
1	large orange

Preheat oven to 350°F. Butter a 9-inch ovenproof pie dish. Pour the milk into a saucepan and add the vanilla bean. Set the pan over moderate heat and heat just until bubbles form around the edges. Remove pan from heat, cover, and set aside to infuse for 20 minutes. Remove vanilla bean, wipe dry, and save for future use. Reserve scalded milk.

Break the whole eggs and egg yolks into a large heat-proof bowl. Add the sugar. Half-fill a large saucepan with boiling water and set the bowl over the saucepan, making sure the bottom of the bowl does not touch the water. Place the pan over moderately low heat. Beat the eggs and sugar with a whisk or rotary beater until thick and pale. Remove the bowl from the pan of water. Stirring the egg mixture constantly with a wooden spoon, gradually pour in the scalded milk in a thin stream. Strain the custard into the prepared pie dish. Set the pie dish in a larger container (such a roasting pan) and pour in enough boiling water to reach halfway up the sides of the pie dish. Bake the custard for 40 to 50 minutes, or until a knife inserted in the center comes out clean. Remove the baked custard from the water bath.

Increase oven temperature to 425°F. Spoon the orange-flavored liqueur over the top of the custard. Spread the meringue over the custard in decorative swirls. Return the pie dish to the oven and bake for 5 minutes, until the meringue has browned slightly and is streaked with gold. Grate the rind from the orange and sprinkle it over the top of the meringue. Serve the custard immediately if you are serving it hot; or cool at room temperature and chill before serving.

Almond and Apricot Meringue Cake

6 portions

2	cups lukewarm tea
4	ounces dried apricots
4	egg whites
⅛	teaspoon cream of tartar
⅛	teaspoon salt
1⅛	cups superfine sugar
3	teaspoons lemon juice, or 1 teaspoon vinegar and 2 teaspoons lemon juice

1	teaspoon vanilla extract
3	ounces blanched almonds, ground
4	tablespoons granulated sugar
½	cup cold water
1	cup heavy cream
1	ounce semisweet or unsweetened chocolate

Strain the tea of any leaves and soak the apricots in it for 8 hours or overnight.

Drop the egg whites into a large bowl and let them come to room temperature. Line two 8-inch loose-bottomed pans or two baking sheets with cooking parchment or oiled aluminum foil. Preheat the oven to 275°F. Beat the egg whites until foamy, add the cream of tartar and salt, and beat until whites are thick and close in texture. Add superfine sugar, 1 teaspoon at a time, making sure all sugar is dissolved before adding more. Whisk 1 teaspoon lemon juice or the vinegar and the vanilla into the meringue. Using a metal spoon or a rubber spatula, fold in the ground almonds, using a figure-eight movement. Divide the meringue equally between the cake pans or spread into two 8-inch rounds on the baking sheets. Bake for 50 minutes, or until lightly colored and set.

Turn the apricots and their soaking liquid into a heavy pan and simmer for 15 minutes. Spoon the granulated sugar into another heavy pan and add the cold water and the remaining 2 teaspoons lemon juice. Stir, bring to a boil, and boil the syrup for 2 minutes. Remove from heat and cool. Purée the simmered apricots in a blender or food processor. Whip the cream until stiff. Fold one third of the apricot purée into two thirds of the whipped cream. Stir the remaining apricot purée into the cold lemon syrup to make a sauce. Set apricot cream, remaining whipped cream and sauce aside.

When the meringues are baked, gently peel the paper from the bases. Cool the layers. Sandwich the layers together with the apricot-flavored cream. Pipe remaining plain whipped cream on top in a decorative fashion. Grate the chocolate and sprinkle a little on the cream swirls. Serve the apricot sauce separately.

Boules de Neige au Chocolat

(Meringue "Eggs" in Chocolate Custard)

This is a chocolate version of oeufs à la neige.

6 portions

2½ cups milk	3 tablespoons powdered
1 teaspoon vanilla extract	cocoa
1 cup superfine sugar	4 egg yolks
2 egg whites	

Pour the milk into a heavy shallow saucepan and add the vanilla and 4 tablespoons of the sugar. Simmer over low heat, stirring occasionally, until the sugar is dissolved. Beat the egg whites in a mixing bowl until they are thick and close in texture. Beat 1 tablespoon of the sugar into the egg whites for 1 minute. Then, using a metal spoon or rubber spatula, carefully fold 7 tablespoons of the sugar into the meringue. Bring the sweetened milk to a steady slow simmer. Use a large spoon to scoop up the meringue and drop a few balls of it into the simmering milk. Simmer for 4 to 5 minutes, stirring the milk once and turning the meringue "eggs" once to cook all sides. As they are done, carefully lift meringues from the milk and set them on paper towels to drain. Continue until

all the meringue is used. Strain the milk and keep warm over low heat.

To make the custard, place the remaining 4 tablespoons sugar, the powdered cocoa and the egg yolks in a mixing bowl and beat to combine. Gradually stir in the strained hot milk. Place the mixing bowl over a pan of barely simmering water, making sure the water does not touch the bottom of the bowl. Cook the custard, stirring constantly with a wooden spoon, until it is thick enough to coat the spoon (see Volume 11 Index). Remove custard from heat and let it cool slightly for a few minutes.

Pour the chocolate custard into a glass serving bowl or individual sundae glasses. Carefully place the meringues on top. Chill in the refrigerator for at least 2 hours.

Meringue Crown

6 portions

1	Meringue Basket, 8 inches in diameter
1	recipe Butter Icing, flavored with orange (see Volume 1 Index)
½	cup chopped pistachios
⅓	cup chopped candied angelica
⅓	cup halved glacé cherries
1	to 1½ pints vanilla ice cream

Place the baked and cooled meringue basket on a flat serving plate. Spread the top edge of the basket with a little of the butter icing. Spread remaining butter icing over the outside of the basket. Lightly press the pistachios and angelica into the icing around the sides and top edge, making a design.

Press the glacé cherry halves into the icing at regular intervals to suit the design. Use an ice-cream scoop to shape balls of ice cream and fill the basket with the ice cream, scooping until the basket is full. Mound the balls in the center of the basket so they peep over the top.

Meringue Almond Layer Cake

4 to 6 portions

8	tablespoons plus 2 teaspoons butter
1	cup all-purpose flour
1	teaspoon baking powder
	salt
2	cups confectioners' sugar
4	egg yolks
½	teaspoon almond extract
2	tablespoons milk (optional)
2	egg whites
	pinch of cream of tartar
½	cup superfine sugar
½	cup toasted slivered almonds

Filling

4 tablespoons unsalted butter	2 tablespoons Coffee
1 cup confectioners' sugar	Essence (see Volume 1
⅛ teaspoon salt	Index)
½ teaspoon vanilla extract	

Preheat oven to 350°F. Use the 2 teaspoons of butter to coat two 7-inch loose-bottomed cake pans. Sift the flour, baking powder and ⅛ teaspoon salt together. Cream the remaining 8 tablespoons butter in a mixing bowl. Sift in the confectioners' sugar; cream the butter and sugar together with a wooden spoon until light and fluffy. Beat in the eggs yolks, one at a time, adding 1 tablespoon of the sifted flour mixture with each yolk. Fold in the remaining flour, beating until all ingredients are well blended. Stir in the almond extract and, if necessary, 1 or 2 tablespoons of milk to give the batter a pouring consistency (do not thin it too much). Pour half of the batter into each of the prepared pans.

In another mixing bowl, beat the egg whites until foamy, add the cream of tartar and a pinch of salt, and beat until they form soft peaks. Gradually add the superfine sugar, beating constantly, and continue beating until the meringue forms stiff peaks. With a spatula, spread the meringue evenly over the batter in one of the cake pans. Sprinkle the almonds evenly over the meringue.

Bake both cake layers for 25 minutes, until a skewer inserted in the centers of the cakes comes out clean. The meringue-topped layer may need an extra 10 minutes. Cool the layers in the pans for 10 minutes, then remove from the pans and cool them completely on a wire rack.

Make the filling: In a large mixing bowl, cream the 4 tablespoons butter with the back of a wooden spoon until soft. Gradually sift in half of the sugar and add the salt. Cream the mixture together until it is pale and fluffy. Mix in the vanilla extract and coffee essence, and sift in remaining sugar. Beat to combine thoroughly. With a spatula, spread the filling over the cake layer without the meringue topping. Place the meringue-topped cake over the filling. Serve at once.

Galettes de Feuilles

(Meringue Leaves)

25 cookies

3	egg whites	½	cup ground blanched almonds
	pinch of cream of tartar	¼	teaspoon almond extract
	pinch of salt	3	ounces semisweet cooking chocolate
6	tablespoons superfine sugar		

Preheat oven to 350°F. Let the egg whites come to room temperature in a large mixing bowl. Line two baking sheets with cooking parchment or oiled aluminum foil. Beat the egg whites with a whisk or rotary beater until frothy. Add cream of tartar and salt. Beat until dissolved. Beat in the sugar, 1 tablespoon at a time, and continue beating until the mixture is smooth and holds stiff peaks. Stir in the ground almonds and almond extract. Drop teaspoons of the meringue on the foil or paper, about 12 meringues to a baking sheet. Bake the galettes for 10 to 15 minutes, until they are set and golden brown on top. Halfway through the baking time, reverse the position of the baking sheets.

Remove baking sheets from the oven and lift off the paper with the galettes. Place the paper, meringue side down, on a large wire rack. Allow the galettes to cool, then carefully peel off the foil or paper. Set the cookies aside to cool completely.

Break the chocolate into small pieces and place it in a small heatproof bowl. Set the bowl in a saucepan containing enough hot water to come halfway up the sides of the bowl. Place the saucepan over moderate heat and melt the chocolate, stirring constantly. Lift the bowl from the hot water and cool the chocolate a little. With a table knife or very thin spatula, spread chocolate on the smooth side of each galette. When the chocolate has almost set, mark leaf veins with a skewer. Cool the cookies so the chocolate becomes firm. Store in an airtight container, but do not refrigerate.

Chestnut Vacherin

6 portions

6	egg whites	1	teaspoon vanilla extract
¼	teaspoon cream of tartar	1	cup heavy cream
¼	teaspoon salt	1¼	cups sweetened chestnut purée*
1⅝	cups superfine sugar		
2	teaspoons lemon juice or vinegar	4	candied chestnuts (marrons glacés)*
1½	tablespoons cornstarch		

Place the egg whites in a very large bowl and let come to room temperature. Preheat oven to 275°F. Prepare two 8-inch loose-bottomed cake pans and 1 baking sheet by lining them with cooking parchment or oiled aluminum foil. Whisk the egg whites until foamy, add cream of tartar and salt, and whisk until whites are thick and close in texture. Whisk in the sugar, 1 teaspoon at a time, making sure each addition is dissolved before adding the next. Whisk in the lemon juice or vinegar, cornstarch and vanilla, and continue to whisk until the meringue is thick and glossy. Fit a pastry bag with a 1-inch star tip and fill the bag with the meringue. Use one third of the meringue to pipe 6 shells on the prepared baking sheet. Divide the remaining meringue equally between the cake pans; smooth the tops with a spatula. Bake the shells and layers for 50 minutes, or until set.

Whip the cream until stiff. Mix the chestnut purée with two thirds of the whipped cream and reserve the rest. When the meringues are baked, gently peel away the paper on the bottom and cool both shells and layers. Sandwich the meringue layers with the chestnut cream. Attach the shells to the top layer with a little whipped cream. Use remaining plain whipped cream to decorate the cake. Slice the chestnuts and arrange the slices around the top of the cake.

*Both chestnut purée and candied chestnuts can be obtained in supermarkets and specialty food shops.

Queen of Puddings

6 portions

2½	cups milk		4	ounces dry spongecake
4	tablespoons unsalted butter			pinch of cream of tartar
1	lemon			pinch of salt
10	tablespoons superfine sugar		3	tablespoons strawberry or apricot jam
2	eggs			

Preheat oven to 350°F. Pour the milk into a saucepan and add the butter. Remove the lemon rind with a swivel peeler and add to the milk. Bring mixture just to a boil over medium heat. Remove from heat and add 2 tablespoons of the sugar to the scalded milk. Stir for 2 minutes to dissolve the sugar. Cover and leave to infuse for 10 minutes. Squeeze the juice from the lemon and add to the milk.

Separate the eggs and set the whites aside to come to room temperature. Butter a 4-cup baking dish. Reduce the dry cake to crumbs and put crumbs in the buttered baking dish. Beat the egg yolks; add a little of the scalded milk, then pour into the rest of the milk. Strain the mixture onto the cake crumbs. Stir well, so all the crumbs are saturated. Place the baking dish in the center of the oven and bake for 20 minutes, or until set.

Beat the egg whites, add cream of tartar and salt, and beat until they are thick and close in texture. Add 4 tablespoons of the sugar, 1 tablespoon at a time, and beat in until dissolved. Fold in the rest of the sugar. Remove pudding from the oven and increase oven temperature to 400°F. Spread the jam over the top of the pudding. Cover with the meringue, spreading it from the middle. Bake in the center of the oven for 10 minutes, or until the meringue is golden.

Salzburger Nockerln

(Austrian Meringues)

4 portions

2	whole eggs
2	egg whites
1	teaspoon vanilla extract
1	lemon
1	tablespoon flour

	pinch of cream of tartar
	pinch of salt
1	cup superfine sugar
1	tablespoon confectioners' sugar

Preheat oven to 350°F. Separate the whole eggs. Put all the egg whites in a large bowl and the yolks in another; let the whites come to room temperature. Using a fork, beat the vanilla extract into the egg yolks. Grate the lemon rind to measure 1 teaspoon and add to the yolks. Sift the flour and beat in with a fork. Whisk the egg whites until foamy, add cream of tartar and salt, and whisk until whites are thick and close in texture. Whisk in ½ cup of the superfine sugar, 1 tablespoon at a time, until whites are very stiff. Fold in remaining sugar, half at a time. Using a spatula or metal spoon, stir about 2 tablespoons of the meringue into the egg yolks, then fold the yolk mixture into the rest of the meringue.

Butter an oval ovenproof dish. Pile the batter into the dish in four mounds, not touching each other. Bake in the center of the oven for 10 to 12 minutes, until brown on the outside but still soft on the inside. Sift confectioners' sugar over the *nockerln* and serve immediately.

Meringue Walnut Torte

6 portions

3	egg whites	1	cup superfine sugar
12	soda crackers with unsalted tops	1	cup ground walnuts
	pinch of cream of tartar	1	teaspoon vanilla extract
	pinch of salt	1	teaspoon baking powder
		¾	cup heavy cream

Preheat oven to 350°F. Bring the whites to room temperature in a large mixing bowl. Brush an 8-inch round cake pan with vegetable oil. Crush the crackers to fine crumbs. Beat the egg whites until foamy, add cream of tartar and salt, and beat until they are thick and close in texture. Add 1 tablespoon of the sugar and continue beating for 1 minute. With a metal spoon or rubber spatula, carefully and thoroughly fold in remaining sugar, the walnuts, vanilla, cracker crumbs and baking powder. Spoon the mixture into the cake pan. Bake the torte in the center of the oven for 30 minutes.

Whip the cream until stiff and chill until ready to serve. Remove the torte from the oven and cool it completely before serving. Serve straight from the pan, with the whipped cream alongside.

Vacherin à l'Orange et Citron

(Orange and Lemon Meringue Cake)

6 to 8 portions

5	egg whites	2	egg yolks
1	lemon	2	drops of orange food coloring (optional)
¼	teaspoon cream of tartar	1	tablespoon orange-flavored liqueur (for example, Grand Marnier, Cointreau, or Triple Sec)
¼	teaspoon salt		
1¼	cups superfine sugar		
½	teaspoon lemon extract		
4	oranges	2	tablespoons heavy cream
6	tablespoons unsalted butter		
3	cups confectioners' sugar		

Let the egg whites come to room temperature in a large mixing bowl. Preheat oven to 300°F. With a pencil, draw a 9-inch circle on a piece of cooking parchment or mark it on wax paper. Place the paper on a baking sheet, pencil side down.

Grate the lemon rind to measure 1 teaspoon. Beat egg whites until foamy, add the cream of tartar and salt, and beat until they are thick and close in texture. Beat in ¼ cup of the sugar, 1 tablespoon at a time, until the mixture is thick and glossy. Using a metal spoon or rubber spatula, fold in remaining sugar, the lemon rind and lemon extract. The meringue should be stiff but not dry. Spoon one third of the meringue onto the outlined circle to make a layer about ¼ inch thick. Fill a large pastry bag fitted with a 1-inch tip with remaining meringue and pipe it around the edge of the circle in decorative swirls to form a case with low sides. Bake the meringue for 1 hour. Turn off the oven and leave meringue in the oven for 30 minutes longer, until it is crisp on the outside but still soft in the center.

Remove baking sheet from the oven and leave the meringue case to cool completely. When cool, lift it off the baking sheet and carefully remove the paper from the bottom.

Make the filling: Grate the rind from half of one of the oranges. Soften the butter, then beat it in a mixing bowl until it is creamy. Add the confectioners' sugar and beat it with the butter until light and fluffy. Stir in the egg yolks and beat well. Stir in orange food coloring, orange rind, liqueur and cream. Mix the ingredients together until thoroughly combined. Spoon the filling into the meringue case, smoothing it with the back of a spoon.

Peel the 4 oranges completely, removing as much white as possible. Slice them, and remove any seeds. Arrange the slices on top of the vacherin and serve it immediately.

Part Five

A LATE-NIGHT SUPPER FOR TWO

"After a perfect meal we are more susceptible to the ecstasy of love than at any other time."

Dr. Hans Balzli
Quoted in Evan Jones, ed., *A Food Lover's Companion* (1979)

What ignites our romantic fantasies more quickly than the thought of a late-night supper for two? Whether we see ourselves in a penthouse floating above the harsh realities of the streets or in the wainscotted dining room of the Colonial "saltbox" on the corner of Elm Street, that candlelit dinner has held our imaginations for decades. It comes at us from Hollywood, from Tin Pan Alley, from Madison Avenue, and its potency always makes our hearts go thump. With that in mind, we conceived this dinner as a chance for you to make some of your dreams—at least about this subject—come true.

It is, of course, possible to do such a dinner in myriad ways—like William Powell and Myrna Loy with silver pails of beluga caviar, a bottle of Dom Perignon and a bunch of baby orchids as a centerpiece, or Rodolfo and Mimi with sausage, rough red wine and a single rose laid across one plate. We have taken a middle course and present here a simple but elegant dinner that will make your love feel cosseted and cherished but won't leave you eating luncheon meat and baked beans for months afterwards.

Since this is a late-night supper, we have made it a light one; and one that despite the elaborate *dacquoise* and the loveliness of the food is easy to prepare. We have assumed that you are going to spend the earlier part of the evening out and that you will want to have as much of the meal as possible ready before you leave. The order of battle, then, should be, more or less, as follows: On the day before your dinner, soak the wild rice and make the meringue layers and the chocolate mousse. The morning of your dinner make the soup, prepare the chicken for cooking, peel the broccoli and slice the mushrooms. Refrigerate all of these, first placing the broccoli in a bowl of cold water. Assemble the dacquoise, cover lightly and set aside at room temperature. Leave everything else until you return home on the evening of your dinner—completing the meal won't take long at all. (Remember that you can make the Maltaise sauce and keep it warm over—not in—hot water while you finish cooking.) Give your love a glass of wine and invite him/her into the kitchen, or let your companion wait for you—ever more eagerly—as the perfumes of this delicious meal invade the living room.

When you create the mood of this dinner try to think of the things the person you are doing this for likes best—your lover, husband, boyfriend, girlfriend, or wife's favorite color, flower, music. If she or he likes napkin rings and sterling, try to use them; if Al Jarreau, Mantovani and/or Bach, play them; if antiques and collectibles, use a few as table decorations. Be sure to put out a few of your favorite things, too. There should be a whisper of your togetherness everywhere you turn. If you like, leave a small gift beside your loved one's plate.

Thomas Wolfe, who no doubt had never had his consciousness raised, once wrote: "There is no spectacle on earth more appealing than that of a beautiful woman in the act of cooking dinner for the man she loves." The fact is that cooking—done by whichever sex—is, or rather should be, at all times an act of love, and on this night more than on most others, you have the opportunity to make it one.

Meursault

Despite its amusing name, which translates as "mouse jump," Meursault, from the Côte de Beaune region of Burgundy, is one of the fine white wines of France. Unlike some of the flintier French wines, Chablis, for example, Meursault is soft, supple and opulent. Typically a medium-bodied dry wine marked unmistakably by the rich flavor and fragrance of the Chardonnay grape, it has a unique and complex quality with tones of vanilla, wood, and, sometimes, almond rounding out its taste.

Meursaults are readily available in fine wine stores. For the very best (and at a price to match) look for Grievault, made from grapes grown in the heart of the finest of the Meursault vineyards—the Perrières. Also excellent is Drouhin. But it is not necessary to spend that much to have a beautiful Meursault. Try Michelot Buisson or Pierre Boillot for medium-priced examples of the wine and, at a slightly lower cost, the wines of Pierre Matrot and Ropiteau Frères.

DINNER FOR TWO

Chicken, Clam and Tomato Broth
Breast of Chicken Stuffed with Curried Mousse
Broccoli with Sauce Maltaise
Wild Rice with Sautéed Mushrooms
Chocolate Dacquoise

MARKET LIST

Meat

1   large chicken breast, boned, skinned and split (about 9 ounces)

Produce

garlic
1   pound broccoli
2   lemons

Dairy

10   tablespoons unsalted butter
6   eggs
heavy cream

¼   pound mushrooms
dill
parsley

Staples

unsweetened cocoa
1   cup homemade chicken stock or 1 can (13¾ ounces) canned broth
cornstarch
tomato juice

frozen orange juice
vegetable oil
cream of tartar
dillweed
cayenne pepper
black pepper

white pepper
curry powder
salt
confectioners' sugar
superfine sugar
vanilla extract

Specialty Items

⅓   cup shelled almonds
semisweet chocolate
mango chutney

1   bottle (8 ounces) clam juice
1   box (8 ounces) wild rice

Chicken, Clam and Tomato Broth

2 portions

1	cup Chicken Stock (see Volume 1 Index) or canned broth
1	cup bottled clam juice
1	cup tomato juice
1	teaspoon snipped fresh dill, or ½ teaspoon dried dillweed

1	garlic clove
1	lemon
	salt and freshly ground pepper
1	teaspoon minced parsley

Combine the chicken stock, clam juice and tomato juice in a saucepan set over moderate heat. Add the snipped dill. Peel the garlic clove and add it to the soup. Grate the lemon rind to measure 1 teaspoon and set it aside. Squeeze the lemon until you have 2 teaspoons of juice. Add the juice to the soup. Simmer the soup for about 10 minutes. Discard the garlic.

Season the soup to taste with salt and pepper. If not serving immediately, partly cover and set aside.

When ready to serve, reheat the soup if necessary. Serve sprinkled with the reserved lemon rind and minced parsley.

Breast of Chicken Stuffed with Curried Mousse

2 portions

1	large chicken breast, boned, skinned and split (about 8 or 9 ounces)
1½	teaspoons egg white
1	tablespoon heavy cream

	salt and freshly ground pepper
⅛	to ¼ teaspoon curry powder
1	tablespoon unsalted butter
1	tablespoon vegetable oil
	mango chutney

Remove the small fillet from each breast half, pulling out the white tendon. If boning the chicken breast yourself (see Volume 9 Index), save the little bits of chicken that adhere to the bones and add them to the fillets. Combine the fillets with the egg white and cream and purée in a food processor, or mince the chicken very fine and combine with the egg white,

omitting the cream. Add salt, pepper and curry powder to taste and process briefly or mix to blend.

Place a breast half flat on a work surface and use a thin, sharp knife to cut across the breast, parallel to the work surface, being careful not to cut all the way through the breast—it should open like a book. Open up the breast and place 2 tablespoons of the reserved mousse as far into the breast as possible. Fold the top of the breast over the bottom, smoothing it down. Refrigerate for several hours.

Heat the butter and oil in a heavy skillet and sauté the chicken breast halves for about 3 minutes over moderate heat. Turn them and sauté for about 3 minutes more, or until the chicken is a very pale gold and the juices run clear. Remove to a heated serving platter and garnish with a spoonful or two of mango chutney.

Broccoli with Sauce Maltaise

Sauce Maltaise is an orange-flavored hollandaise.

2 portions

1	pound broccoli
2	teaspoons salt

Sauce Maltaise (recipe follows)

Remove the tough bottom stems of the broccoli and separate the broccoli into small bunches. Peel the stems, starting at the bottom and peeling upward. If not cooking immediately, place broccoli in a bowl of cold water and refrigerate.

Bring 3 quarts of water to a boil, add the salt, and plunge the broccoli into the water. Cook, uncovered, for about 6 minutes or until broccoli is bright green and barely tender. Drain the broccoli and place on a heated serving plate. Spoon a small amount of sauce over the broccoli and serve the rest of the sauce separately.

Sauce Maltaise

makes about ¾ cup

8	tablespoons unsalted butter
1	lemon
3	egg yolks
1	tablespoon undiluted frozen orange juice

½	teaspoon salt
	freshly ground white pepper
	pinch of cayenne pepper

Using these ingredients, follow the recipe given in Volume 3 for Hollandaise Sauce, or follow the food processor/blender directions given below.

In a heavy saucepan set over medium heat, melt the butter until it is bubbling. Do not let it brown.

Squeeze the lemon to measure 1 tablespoon juice. Place the egg yolks, lemon and orange juice, and salt and peppers in a food processor or blender and process for 3 or 4 seconds. Scrape down the sides and process for 2 or 3 seconds longer. Remove the plunger from the feed tube or the insert on the blender lid and, with the motor running, let the melted butter trickle as slowly as possible into the egg yolks. After all the butter has been added, the sauce should be thick. Transfer it to a serving bowl, partly cover, and set it over—not in—hot water to keep it warm until serving time.

Wild Rice with Sautéed Mushrooms

This long-hot-soak method of cooking wild rice pre-serves its delicate flavor. If you are not going to be home the day of your dinner, the wild rice can be started the evening before and left to cool overnight. The second application of boiling water can then be done in the morning and the wild rice left all day, if necessary.

2 portions

⅓ cup wild rice	1 tablespoon unsalted butter
salt	freshly ground pepper
¼ pound mushrooms	

Wash wild rice in cold water and drain it. Place it in a heavy saucepan with a tight-fitting lid. In a separate kettle, bring to a boil sufficient water to fill the pot containing the wild rice. Pour the boiling water over the wild rice, filling the pot, cover, and set aside. Do not uncover at any time. When the water has cooled completely, which will take about 3 hours, drain the wild rice and repeat the procedure with fresh boiling water to which a teaspoon of salt has been added. After another 3 hours, the wild rice will be fully open. Drain it and set aside.

Wipe the mushrooms with a damp cloth or paper towel. Trim the stems and slice the mushrooms. Melt the butter in a heavy skillet and sauté the mushrooms for 3 or 4 minutes, stirring frequently, until they start to give up their juices. Add the wild rice, tossing to mix with the mushrooms. Add salt and pepper to taste and heat gently. Stir occasionally.

Chocolate Dacquoise

The meringue layers for this cake can be baked several days in advance and stored in an airtight container.

2 portions

3 egg whites	1 tablespoon cornstarch
⅛ teaspoon cream of tartar	2 tablespoons unsweetened cocoa
1 teaspoon vanilla extract	Chocolate Mousse Filling
¾ cup superfine sugar	(recipe follows)
⅓ cup shelled almonds	

Butter and flour a large baking sheet. Mark on it six rectangles, each measuring 4 × 5 inches. Set the sheet aside. Preheat the oven to 325°F.

Beat the egg whites until foamy, add the cream of tartar, and beat until soft peaks form. Beat in the vanilla and gradually add ½ cup of the sugar, 1 tablespoon at a time, beating continuously. Beat until the meringue is thick and close in texture.

Pulverize the almonds in a food processor or nut grinder. You should have about ¼ cup. Sift the cornstarch with the cocoa and combine them with the ground almonds and remaining ¼ cup sugar. Fold this mixture into the meringue. Either spread the meringue within the outlines on the baking sheet, evening it out with a spatula, or pipe the meringue through a pastry bag fitted with a large plain tube. Start at the center of the marked rectangle and pipe around and around until the rectangle is completely filled. Bake in the middle level of the oven for about 40 minutes.

To assemble the cake, place two meringue rectangles on a flat surface. Cut eight strips of wax paper, lay them parallel to the sides of each layer and slip them partway under the four edges of each rectangle so there's a border of wax paper all the way around. Spread chocolate mousse evenly on the bottom layers, top with a second layer, spread second layers with mousse and top with third layers. If you have run out of mousse, sift confectioners' sugar over the top layers.

Chocolate Mousse Filling

This delicious chocolate filling can be prepared the night before.

2	eggs		1	tablespoon confectioners' sugar
3	ounces semisweet chocolate		¼	cup heavy cream, chilled
	pinch of cream of tartar		¼	teaspoon vanilla extract

Separate the eggs and let the whites come to room temperature. Melt the chocolate in the top of a double boiler set over hot water. Remove from the heat and stir until smooth; let cool slightly. Beat in the egg yolks, one at a time. Transfer the mixture to a large mixing bowl. In a separate bowl beat the whites until they are soft and foamy and add the cream of tartar. Gradually add the sugar, beating until soft peaks form.

Whip the cream until thick but not stiff, beating in the vanilla as it thickens.

Fold one third of the egg whites into the chocolate mixture to lighten it. Then gently fold in the balance of the whites and the whipped cream until the mousse is smooth and only a few white streaks remain. Cover and refrigerate at least 6 hours or overnight.

INDEX